THE OLD
FARMER'S
ALMANAC

CONTAINER GARDENER'S HANDBOOK

This book is dedicated to the 13th editor of *The Old Farmer's Almanac* and
editor of the *Gardener's Handbook* series, Janice Stillman,
with gratitude and appreciation for her contributions over 23 years.

The Old Farmer's Almanac Books
PUBLISHER: Sherin Pierce
EDITOR: Janice Stillman
CREATIVE DIRECTOR: Colleen Quinnell
MANAGING EDITOR: Jack Burnett
EDITORIAL STAFF: Carol Connare, Tim Goodwin, Sarah Perreault, Heidi Stonehill

V.P., NEW MEDIA AND PRODUCTION: Paul Belliveau
PRODUCTION DIRECTOR: David Ziarnowski
PRODUCTION MANAGER: Brian Johnson
PRODUCTION ARTISTS: Jennifer Freeman, Rachel Kipka, Janet Selle

SENIOR DIGITAL EDITOR: Catherine Boeckmann
ASSOCIATE DIGITAL EDITOR: Jennifer Keating
SENIOR WEB DESIGNER: Amy O'Brien
DIGITAL MARKETING SPECIALISTS: Jessica Garcia, Holly Sanderson
E-MAIL MARKETING SPECIALIST: Eric Bailey
E-COMMERCE MARKETING DIRECTOR: Alan Henning
SENIOR DRUPAL DEVELOPER: Mark Gordon

CONTRIBUTORS: Steve Bender, Doreen G. Howard, Mare-Anne Jarvela,
Martie Majoros, Robin Sweetser, Gayla Trail

COVER PHOTO CREDITS: See page 208 for credits from Edibles and Ornamentals profiles.
BACK COVER PHOTOS, CLOCKWISE FROM TOP LEFT: ejkrouse/Getty Images;
Parkin Srihawong/Shutterstock; Antony-Kemp/Getty Images; sagarmanis/Getty Images;
Tatjana Michaljova/Shutterstock; Udo Kroener/Shutterstock

Special thanks to Proven Winners for use of their extensive image library.

For additional information about this and other publications from
The Old Farmer's Almanac, visit ALMANAC.COM or call 1-800-ALMANAC.

Distributed in the book trade by HarperCollins in the United States and by Firefly Books Ltd. in Canada.

Yankee Publishing Inc., P.O. Box 520, 1121 Main Street, Dublin, New Hampshire 03444

Thank you for buying this book! Thanks, too, to everyone who had a hand in it,
including printers, distributors, and sales and delivery people.

ISBN: 978-1-57198-967-3
First Edition
Printed in China by C. J. Printing Media Co.

COLEUS, EUPHORBIA, AND BEGONIA BRIGHTEN A SHADY CORNER.

PLOTTING YOUR POTTING

Hello, friends! Love to grow plants but think that you have too little space—or maybe none available at all? Try putting your garden plot in a pot! You can grow almost anything in containers—vegetables, herbs, and fruit, as well as a wide array of ornamental plants—and do it almost anywhere!

We've created this *Container Gardener's Handbook* for folks with all levels of experience and widely varying interests because growing in containers is different from growing in-ground or even in raised beds. For example, new "rules" apply: Ordinary "dirt" won't do, and special mixes are recommended; container size is critical; watering needs are greater; and specific "mini" varieties of plants are often recommended.

There's much more to this, of course, and you'll find advice and guidance about all of it on these pages. We believe—no, we know!—that this book will enable you to enjoy very successful container gardening. In fact, you may grow your best "garden" ever—of any type!

Have fun! With this extensive guide, you'll find it easy to "contain" your gardening enthusiasm for all the world to see!

–*Janice Stillman*

A BALCONY COMES ALIVE
WITH GROW BAGS CONTAINING
TOMATOES, HOT PEPPERS,
STRAWBERRIES, MARIGOLDS,
AND MORE.

CONTENTS

PART 1

Whether for pots or plots, *The Old Farmer's Almanac*
Garden Planner is easy-to-use yet super-sophisticated
software for any device—even your phone! Start
a free 7-day trial today (no credit card required!)
at GardenPlanner.Almanac.com.

EVEN THE SMALLEST
SPACE CAN BE
TURNED INTO A CONTAINER
GARDEN HAVEN.

CONTENTS
PART 2

CONTAIN YOURSELF

A STRIKING ARRAY OF POTS INCLUDES EUPHORBIA, HYDRANGEA, PETUNIA, SILVER NICKEL VINE, VERBENA, AND WISHBONE FLOWER.

9

CONTAINERS 101

GARDENING IS LIKE LANDSCAPE PAINTING
TO ME. THE GARDEN IS THE CANVAS. PLANTS, CONTAINERS,
AND OTHER GARDEN FEATURES ARE THE
COLORS. I PAINT ON THE GARDEN OF CANVAS, HOPING
TO CREATE A MASTERPIECE WITH MY COLORS.

–*Ama H. Vanniarachchy, Sri Lankan writer*

It is said that anything that holds a growing medium (e.g., potting mix), provides sufficient room for roots, and drains well can be a plant container. This may be true, but other matters are important, too. When choosing containers for your plants, you need to be cognizant not only of their material composition, size, and drainage capacity but also of other characteristics.

CONTAINER MATERIALS

The most common traditional plant pots are terra-cotta (or clay), glazed ceramic, plastic, and wood. More recently developed materials for the purpose include metal, concrete, landscape fabric, resin, fiberglass, and fiberstone. Each type has advantages and shortcomings.

■ **Terra-cotta pots**—of unglazed red clay—are the classic plant container. These are porous (water permeates them), so roots are less likely to drown, but this also means that they dry out relatively quickly, so plants in them require watering more frequently, especially in warm weather. They are also heavy (to bear in mind if moving

may be required), and they break easily. For example, if terra-cotta pots are left outdoors in winter with soil in them, moisture in the soil will freeze and expand and often cause the pots to crack. Don't like the color? Paint them.

■ **Glazed ceramic pots,** usually more decorative than terra-cotta, may be slightly sturdier than terra-cotta and tend to be nonporous but retain many of terra-cotta's less appealing properties—for example, its weight, fragility, and winter vulnerability.

■ **Plastic pots** are lightweight and thus easy to lift; nonporous, so watering tends to be less frequent; and available in many colors, for ease of aesthetic appeal. Those with saucers attached catch water runoff and tend to be neater than those without but note that standing water is unhealthy for some plants. Plastic pots can be used as

WOOD NOTS

When growing edible crops, avoid containers (including raised beds) made of . . .

• pressure-treated wood: The pesticides and chemicals used in it to prevent damage by pests can leach into the soil and thus your plants.

• railway ties: These are treated with creosote, a toxin.

• plastic lumber: The composites used to make it may not be safe for plants.

liners for terra-cotta pots, thus reducing the clay's porosity somewhat. However, plastic pots absorb heat, which may threaten plants' viability. Also, extended sun exposure can cause the plastic to deteriorate.

■ **Wooden containers** made of cedar or redwood resist decay naturally and last for years, especially if the inside is coated with a nontoxic preservative.

half-barrel easier to move, whether empty or full. Lifting it off of the ground in this way will also help to prevent rot by allowing it to drain.

■ **Galvanized metal containers,** such as feed troughs, are relatively lightweight and frost- and sunproof. They seldom have drainage holes; you need to add them. Note that these

sunproof, but they are usually very heavy and can crack under certain conditions. For the look without the weight, get creative and make your own. Hypertufa, which is made with Portland cement and aggregates, is somewhat lighter than cement and can be formed into almost any shape.

■ **Grow bags** tend to be made from landscape fabric—

SENECIO AND SEDUM, A COOL COLOR COMBO
FOR YEAR-ROUND INTEREST

CANNA AND ELDERBERRY FRESHEN UP A
ROOFTOP OR BALCONY WITH A POP OF COLOR.

Oak half-barrels, originally created to hold wine or whiskey, may last a decade or more and tend to be more watertight than other wooden containers, which is why drainage holes must be drilled into their bottom. Any wooden container is likely to be heavy even when empty, oak half-barrels especially so. Add casters to the bottom to make an oak

are not recommended for growing acidic food crops, such as tomatoes and citrus, as the acid will accelerate corrosion of the zinc coating. Be aware, too, that metal conducts heat, exposing roots to rapid temperature fluctuations that could damage the plants.

■ **Concrete containers** are durable and both frost- and

often of polypropylene or polyethylene—or other feltlike or nonwoven pressed fabrics; you can also find them in burlap or canvas. They are lightweight, come in a wide range of sizes, take shape when filled with soil, can be moved easily (many have handles), and store flat when empty (see page 16 for advice on end-of-season cleaning). Porous, feltlike fabrics (not plastic bags) drain well (through the fabric, without the need for holes) and are breathable: The fabric releases heat during warm spells and insulates plants somewhat on cool evenings. When plant roots touch the side of a grow bag, they are "air-pruned": Roots branch out, so the plants do not become root-bound. Grow bags may require frequent waterings, but because of their porosity, overwatering and root rot are seldom a concern. If you're handy, you can make your own.

■ **Resin containers** are made not from plastic but from an organic compound derived from plants. It is poured into molds to create pots that are lightweight, nonporous, resistant to breaking or cracking, and often blended with UV inhibitors (to resist fading) and can mimic stone or metal in appearance.

■ **Fiberglass containers** usually have a resin core. They are lightweight, rustproof, frost-resistant, shatterproof, and resistant to fading. Avoid containers with bumps, waves, or imperfections in the finish, as these are signs of poor quality. A heavy container may be a sign that fillers were added to the resin.

■ **Fiberstone containers** are made of fiberglass and crushed stone; sand, metal fiber, and other elements may be added for weight and strength. Fiberstone is rigid, durable, and weatherproof. It resembles stone in look and feel and can be made to resemble concrete. Weight varies, based on the materials used and size of a container; fiberstone is heavier than fiberglass.

CONTAINER SIZE

Plants in small containers up to 8 inches in diameter are generally high-maintenance: The smaller the container, the more often the plant will need to be watered. In many cases, this means watering daily, especially if the container is outside. Shallow containers, no matter their width and shape, limit the depth available to plant roots and also usually require frequent waterings. Small containers simply can not store enough moisture to get through hot periods. Large pots insulate plants better.

A plant may outgrow a small container. When moved to a larger pot, the transplant will need a period of time to adjust to its new environment, and doing this introduces the chance that it may fail. To minimize this risk and increase the longevity of the plant in one container, give it enough space to spread. There are no set rules about how much space a plant should have, but here are three recommendations:

1. The diameter of the pot should be at least 1 inch wider than the plant's root mass. If the plant is expected to grow quickly, choose a pot that is up to 4 inches wider than the root mass.

2. Provide an adequate amount of soil under the root ball (about one-third of the

---

VOICES OF EXPERIENCE

I had a three-tiered water fountain that suffered a few cracks during Hurricane Rita. It would no longer hold the water but made a stunning centerpiece in my garden, lined and planted with a variety of herbs and flowers.
–*Ellen J., via Almanac.com*

I once used an antique porcelain bedpan for an indoor plant container (I'm a former nurse). I love to see flowers in old shoes, wheelbarrows, and any antique container. It's interesting to look not only at the flowers/plants but also at the container and wonder about how it was used, who owned it, and so on. I also have used hollowed-out tree stumps for a few pansies or marigolds.
–*Ann H., via Almanac.com*

container height) to allow space for roots to grow. Bring the soil level at the surface up to within 1 to 2 inches of the container's top edge.

3. When choosing a container, consider scale—the pot and the size of your plant at maturity. A simple rule of thumb suggests that the height of the tallest plant(s) should be twice the container's height.

See "Secrets to Growing Food in Containers" (page 44) for specific container sizes for growing fruit, greens, herbs, and vegetables.

CONTAINER DRAINAGE

Adequate drainage is critical to the success of a container garden. Plants breathe through their roots, as well as through leaves, stems, and

containers should never be left to stand in water, why more holes are better than one hole in the bottom of a container, and why it is wise to facilitate drainage and air circulation by raising up a container on a brick or other platform.

One hole in the bottom center of a container is seldom adequate for good drainage. A better arrangement is

SUMMER SNAPDRAGON, CALIBRACHOA, HARDY BABY'S BREATH, PETUNIA, AND WHITE LICORICE

SILVER NICKEL VINE, CALADIUM, AND COLEUS BRIGHTEN UP A SHADY AREA.

For example, if a plant is expected to top out at 4 feet, the container should be 2 feet high.

Containers intended for perennials or shrubs that will be outdoors year-round (not overwintered in a basement or garage, for example) should be significantly larger than the plant's root mass because a container generally reduces a plant's hardiness by two zones.

flowers. In order for the roots to respirate, there must be air in the soil. A proper potting mix that is not too wet will retain air. However, if the soil is too wet—usually because water does not drain off—the cells in the roots will not be able to breathe. If the roots can not breathe, they will die and put the entire plant at risk of dying. This is why

¼- to ½-inch-diameter holes located every 2 to 3 inches in the bottom of the container. (Occasionally, you will see or want to make holes around the bottom of a container's side wall. This can help water to drain away from the container, assuming that the surface on which the container is sitting on does not cause the water to pool.)

MAKE A SELF-WATERING CONTAINER

AN IDEA NEEDS PROPAGATION AS MUCH AS A PLANT NEEDS WATERING. OTHERWISE, BOTH WILL WITHER AND DIE.
–Bhimrao Ramji Ambedkar, Indian political leader (1891–1956)

When the weather gets very hot, how do you keep up with the watering? Just make a self-watering container in six steps—and this chore will be much easier on you and your plants!

You will need:

1 plastic yogurt container, cup, or similar (with lip) to act as a wicking chamber
2 buckets (e.g., 5-gallon, food-grade plastic buckets) that when stacked will leave a gap between the bottom and top buckets, with 1 lid (if desired)
keyhole saw or sturdy utility knife
1-inch-diameter plastic pipe slightly longer than the height of the two stacked buckets
electric drill, with ¼- and ½-inch bits
good-quality potting mix
plant(s)

MAKE A WICKING CHAMBER

Using a marker, trace an outline of the plastic container onto the center of the base of the top bucket. Cut just inside the outline using a keyhole saw (or utility knife); the hole should be ever so slightly smaller than the container, just enough such that the lip of the container does not slip through the hole.

Poke or drill ½-inch-diameter holes all over the sides of the plastic container/wicking chamber to allow water to enter from the reservoir.

When filled with potting mix, the wicking chamber will wick water up from the water reservoir into the top bucket. Make sure that the bottom of your top bucket is high enough off the bottom bucket's bottom to allow the wicking chamber to fit all the way into its hole.

MAKE A WATER DELIVERY PIPE

Cut the pipe to a length that makes it slightly higher than the final soil level of the two stacked buckets.

Cut one end of your plastic pipe to give it a 45-degree angle. This will let the water flow freely from the pipe into the reservoir.

Trace the outline of the pipe onto the base of the top bucket (which has the hole for the wicking chamber) about 2 inches in from the outside edge, then cut it out.

DRILL DRAINAGE HOLES

Drill lots of ¼-inch holes into the base of the top bucket. Use a random pattern or an orderly effect, whichever you prefer.

DRILL AN OVERFLOW HOLE

Insert the top bucket into the bottom bucket. They should not fit snugly. If necessary, set

small cups or plant pots into the bottom bucket to keep the top bucket from resting on the bottom bucket's base. On the exterior of the bottom bucket, use a marker to indicate where the base of the top bucket meets the bottom bucket. Just below this line, drill a ¼-inch hole in the side of the bottom bucket. This is your overflow hole; it will prevent the potting mix in the top bucket from getting waterlogged.

ASSEMBLE YOUR CONTAINER

Insert the top bucket into the bottom bucket. Pack the wicking chamber with potting mix, then set the chamber

SEE HOW IT'S DONE

Seeing is believing, so to better understand how this works, watch a video on how to make this self-watering container at Almanac .com/self-watering-pot.

into its hole in the bottom of the top bucket. Push the water delivery pipe through its hole in the bottom of the top bucket, with the 45-degree-cut end down. Fill the top bucket with potting mix, moistening with water as you fill.

PLANT UP YOUR SELF-WATERING POT

Plant into the potting mix. Cut holes for your plant(s) in a bucket lid to cover up the soil surface and reduce evaporation, which is especially important in hot climates. (Or cover the soil with a thick garbage bag placed down over the buckets and secured by rubber bands, a bungee cord, or string around the outside of the bucket. Cut holes in the bag over the plant[s] and the water delivery pipe.)

Pour water into the water delivery pipe. Stop pouring when the water starts coming out of the overflow hole.

HOW TO CLEAN
CONTAINERS AND TOOLS

**CLEANING ANYTHING INVOLVES MAKING SOMETHING ELSE DIRTY,
BUT ANYTHING CAN GET DIRTY WITHOUT SOMETHING ELSE GETTING CLEAN.**
–Laurence J. Peter, Canadian educator and writer (1919–90)

Proper cleaning and disinfecting of containers and tools requires minimum effort yet can mean the difference between success and failure for containerized plants. Plus, in the case of containers, they will look more attractive!

A thorough scrubbing of used pots will rid them of "hidden" pests and diseases. Containers may harbor lingering bug eggs and disease pathogens that may not be visible to the naked eye. Salt deposits also accumulate in pots, leaving white residue that can cause plant problems. Clean pots at the end of one growing season or the beginning of the next, but do remember to do it so that you will not be disappointed later.

TO DISINFECT CLAY AND PLASTIC POTS

Remove and discard any dead plants and empty the container of potting mix. It can be tempting to reuse the potting mix, but for the healthy growth of next year's plantings, it is best to start with fresh potting mix each spring. If the plants were not diseased, empty the entire container into your compost pile.

Soak each pot in a solution of 10 parts water to 1 part bleach for 10 minutes to 1 hour. (You can substitute vinegar for the bleach if desired, in which case you would soak the pots for a few hours longer.)

Bleach is a harsh chemical, so take precautions: Wear gloves, eye protection, and old clothes. This procedure will kill off bug eggs and disease spores, as well as help to loosen any white, crusty mineral salts that have accumulated.

Scour the pots with a stiff-bristled brush or steel wool to remove algae, mildew, and other deposits. Although the white crust can be difficult to remove from old clay pots, scrub off as much as you can from all types of containers. Plastic is much easier to clean.

Put the pots into a bucket or sink filled with water made soapy with dish detergent. If mineral deposits remain, use a knife to scrape them off.

Rinse the pots thoroughly and then soak them in a bucket of clean water. Rinse again, if desired, and let the pots dry in the sun.

STORING POTS

When the pots are dry, stack and store them. Plastic pots can be stored outside, but make sure that they are covered and out of direct sunlight. Sunlight degrades the plastic over time, making it brittle and causing colored pots to fade.

Store clay and ceramic, or glazed, pots inside. Unglazed clay is porous (it can absorb moisture), which means that winter freezing and thawing can cause such pots to crack.

To stack ceramic pots, wrap them in newspaper for cushioning and to prevent chipping. Glazed pots can crack if left outside in freezing weather. Bring them inside, along with any other types of glass or ceramic yard art.

TO CLEAN GROW BAGS

Remove the soil from fabric "pots" and grow bags. If the bags are too heavy to lift, scoop out some of the potting mix until you can safely dump the rest into a compost pile.

If the bags are clean, allow them to dry in the sun and then fold and store them.

If they are stained, they can be tossed into the washer or soaked in a bucket of water with a bit of laundry detergent and gently scrubbed as needed.

Rinse the fabric pots thoroughly and let them air-dry in the sun. Do not put fabric or grow bags into the dryer!

TO CLEAN AND DISINFECT TOOLS

Simple maintenance will add longevity to your garden tools. Regular (or at the very least, annual) cleaning is advised.

Use a spray hose to remove caked-on growing medium from tools and then a stiff or wire brush to eliminate anything that remains. Wash the tools in soapy water and let them air-dry in the sun.

When disease is suspected, disinfect tools before using on each plant.

There are a number of agents for disinfecting tools, including . . .

■ isopropyl alcohol (70% or higher): Dip, wipe, or spray tools.

■ bleach: Let tools sit in a 10% bleach solution for at least 10 minutes, then rinse well to prevent corrosion. Dry thoroughly.

After disinfecting, apply a light oil to tools to prevent any metal from rusting.

Store tools away from the elements.

No matter what your pots and tools are made of, do not become discouraged if they are not perfectly clean. Just do the best you can!

SOLVING THE MYSTERIES OF POTTING MIX

PEOPLE NEED TO REALIZE HOW POWERFUL THE TRANSFORMATION OF SOIL CAN BE.

–Ron Finley, "gangsta gardener" and teacher in the Los Angeles area

Just as when growing in-ground, the medium into which you set your plants will determine their survival—and your happiness.

Soil in containers or pots needs to be able to provide anchorage for roots as well as be light enough to allow air and water to reach them. Therefore, the potting medium must be lighter and fluffier than ground soil to provide the space needed for air circulation, good drainage, and healthy root growth.

Which should you use, potting mix or potting soil? The answer may surprise you.

GO SOILLESS TO TOIL LESS

Strictly speaking, bagged garden soil, or dirt, is meant for use in or on the ground. It is relatively heavy because it contains a number of ingredients, including clay or sand. What's more, this media may be impure, putting you at risk of introducing weed seeds, pests, and/or diseases to your plants.

The ideal medium for plants in containers and pots is a "soilless" one. This may be called "potting mix," "soilless potting mix," or sometimes even "potting soil." Because these names can be confusing, it's important to carefully read the label on a bag.

A proper "soilless" container mix generally includes three purposeful ingredients: (1) a moisture- and nutrient-retention agent such as peat moss, rice hulls, or coconut coir; (2) pine bark for anchorage; and (3) either perlite or vermiculite, which allow for air space so that the

PEAT MOSS

PINE BARK

VERMICULITE

18

mixture is light and fluffy. Mixes are sterile, so there is no chance of introducing weed seeds, pests, and/ or diseases. Some potting mixes include a slow-release fertilizer. If you use a mix that contains fertilizer, you'll need to adjust the fertilizer that you provide.

TYPICAL POTTING MIX INGREDIENTS AND THEIR KEY CHARACTERISTICS

■ **Bark** consists of partially composted or ground timber scrap. Properties differ, based on the source material; bark dries out more quickly than peat but generally provides good aeration.

■ **Coconut coir, or coir,** a substitute for peat, is constituted from reddish-brown fibers harvested from coconut husks. It has the same water-holding characteristics and porosity as peat moss but when dry is easier to sufficiently moisten. Coir has a near-neutral pH.

■ **Compost** that is prepared

for in-ground gardening is not suitable for containers: It is too heavy for the needed aeration, and its high nutrient level can "burn" plant roots. Try to use only compost that is homemade or specifically created for potting mixes.

■ **Coarse, or builder's, sand** can improve aeration in potting mix and add weight to a top-heavy container. It has a neutral pH and adds little to no fertility to the mix.

■ **Fertilizers** in soilless mixes can act as either a "starter charge"—a small amount of fertilizer that washes out after a few waterings—or a "continuous" (controlled-,

timed-, or slow-release) application. Continuous fertilizers are contained in "prills" (pellets or globules) that release fertilizer when they get wet. (Potting mix that contains prills must be stored dry; if the mix gets wet while bagged, the fertilizer may be released and become concentrated. As a result, it could burn plant roots when used.)

■ **Peat moss, or peat,** is made of partially decayed plant material—usually mosses (such as sphagnum)—that have been submerged without oxygen in wet, acidic (low pH) conditions, like those found in a bog. Harvesting and using it is considered unsustainable and unhealthy for the planet. (See "Pondering Peat Moss," page 22.)

■ **Perlite,** a nontoxic, odorless, and sterile volcanic rock, improves drainage and aeration.

■ **Rice hulls, sterilized,** can be substituted for perlite or vermiculite.

■ **Vermiculite** is a lightweight,

PERLITE

COCONUT COIR

COMPOST

absorbent, pH-neutral mineral that contains some potassium, magnesium, and calcium. It benefits plants by helping them to retain moisture and nutrients in soilless mixes, especially at the root level.

■ **Wetting agents** are chemical substances that help potting mixes to be uniformly moist when watered. Such polymer gels, crystals, or water-absorbing chemicals aid in a soilless mix's moisture retention, thus reducing the need for watering. (Yucca extract is often the agent in organic mixes.)

For best results when planting, wet the potting mix with warm water first. Avoid placing plants in dry mix and then watering them, as moisture will then be inconsistent around their roots.

MAKE YOUR OWN

If you need only a few small containers' worth of potting mix, you may be better off buying it premade. Making your own is usually only economical on a large scale— if you're planting a lot of containers. If this is you, keep these things in mind before you begin making your mix:

■ The lighter your potting mix, the better. Loose and porous mixtures not only reduce the weight of the container, making it easier to move, but also allow for water, fertilizer, and air to reach plant roots more quickly and provide good drainage, which is important for container gardening.

■ Start with the basic recipe below and then add soil sulfur to lower the pH or lime to raise it, according to the needs of your plants. Both additives can typically be found at garden centers.

■ If rapid drainage is needed— as is the case for cacti, succulents, and lavender, for example—add extra sand and perlite.

■ If greater moisture retention is needed—such as for ferns and woodland flowers (like primrose), for instance— add extra vermiculite or coconut coir.

BASIC CONTAINER POTTING MIX RECIPE
You will need:

10 quarts coconut coir
5 quarts perlite
5 quarts vermiculite
5 quarts screened compost or composted cow manure
2 cups fine sand
2 cups slow-release fertilizer pellets

Mix thoroughly. Makes enough to fill two 14-inch tubs or five 12-inch hanging baskets. Double or triple the recipe for bigger containers.

HOW MUCH POTTING MIX DO I NEED?

While potting mix is sold by volume (usually in quarts), pots can be measured by their volume or diameter. Note that container volumes can vary based on diameter and height. To roughly translate container size into quarts of mix, use the quick reference at right.

THE BOTTOM LINER

When the time comes to fill a container, many gardeners wonder what to do about the bottom. Ideas abound, but not

COMMON TYPES, SIZES, AND VOLUMES OF CONTAINERS

DIAMETER/WIDTH	VOLUME
Pots	
8 to 14 inches ("1-gallon")	4 quarts
9½ to 14 inches ("2-gallon")	8 quarts
11 to 21 inches ("3-gallon")	12 quarts
11 to 25 inches ("4-gallon")	16 quarts
12 to 14 inches ("5-gallon")	20 quarts
12 to 24 inches ("6-gallon" to "8-gallon")	24 to 32 quarts
16 to 19 inches ("9-gallon" to "12-gallon")	36 to 48 quarts
Hanging Baskets	
12 inches	6 quarts
16 inches	10 quarts
Window Boxes	
24 inches by 6 inches	12 quarts
36 inches by 6 inches	20 quarts

all of them are recommended. Here are several, with explanations.

■ First, the bottom of a container should have holes for drainage. This is essential for any container, regardless of plant(s). If water does not drain, root rot can occur.

■ Small pots seldom need their drainage holes covered. However, if there is concern about soil spilling out of a pot's drainage hole(s), cut a piece of newspaper or a paper towel to fit in the bottom of the pot. Another option for eliminating or reducing the clogging of a container's drainage holes is to line its bottom with porous landscape fabric or shade cloth.

■ Filling large pots with potting mix can be costly, but you can make a deep one shallow. Cut plywood to fit inside the pot at the depth needed for healthy roots (9 inches or more). Drill hole(s) in it before inserting. If ballast is needed, place a rock or brick in the bottom of the container before putting the plywood in place. Then fill with potting mix as needed.

■ Gravel or small pebbles are often cited as bottom filler because stones add weight to a container and provide additional depth through which water can percolate. Indeed, stones of any size will add weight to a container, but this weight may hinder your ability to move the pot. If greater weight is needed, try planting in a lightweight plastic container that you then insert into a larger, heavier (ceramic, metal, or other) pot. A bottom gravel layer will not improve drainage and may in fact lead to root rot and plant death. The lowest soil in a pot is the most saturated; adding gravel at the bottom raises the wet soil layer, bringing it closer to roots and potentially drowning them.

■ Avoid layering shredded newspaper, cardboard, biodegradable Styrofoam, or packing peanuts made from corn in the bottom of a container, as these materials will eventually become saturated, break down, and form a wet mass that does not drain properly and is impenetrable by roots.

■ Avoid plastic bottles, metal cans, bubble wrap, or other recyclable material, as well as golf balls and grocery bags. As appropriate, recycle these properly instead.

PONDERING PEAT MOSS

IN THE DEPTHS OF THE MOOR, THE PEAT MAY BE SEEN RIVEN LIKE FLOES OF ICE, AND THE RIFTS ARE SOMETIMES TWELVE TO FOURTEEN FEET DEEP, CUT THROUGH BLACK VEGETABLE MATTER, THE PRODUCT OF DECAY OF PLANTS THROUGH COUNTLESS GENERATIONS.
–Sabine Baring-Gould, English priest and writer (1834–1924)

For years, gardeners have used peat moss and peat-based soilless mixes. In fact, it's hard not to use peat in some gardening projects—but this is increasingly frowned upon. Read on to learn about peat, plus alternatives that you can use and why you might consider them.

WHAT IS PEAT MOSS?

Peat moss, or "peat," is made of partially decayed plant material. Its main component is usually sphagnum moss, but it also may contain the detritus of reeds, sedges, heather, and carnivorous plants—all of which having been submerged without oxygen in wet, acidic conditions, like those found in a bog. This decaying process is very slow, taking up to 1,000 years to create a 36-inch layer, for example. For centuries, peat was used in the United Kingdom and elsewhere as heating fuel; more recently, it has become fuel for power

plants, some of which are trying to reclaim and replant the bogs—although it is virtually impossible to regenerate and replicate these sensitive habitats. (The sale of horticultural peat to gardeners in the UK is banned as of 2024.)

For the harvest or mining of peat, the bogs are first drained, after which the peat is scraped off or vacuumed up. Peat bogs are some of our largest carbon stores on the planet, holding 30% of the world's soil carbon. Harvesting it releases this CO_2 into the atmosphere.

Most of the peat sold in North America comes from Canada. Our northern neighbor has some 280,000,000 acres of peatlands, about .03% of which have been harvested. About .05% of what is harvested goes to horticultural use. The industry in Canada is relatively young and operates under strict

governmental controls, which require replanting and restoring the water table in any drained area.

However, re-creating a natural ecosystem such as a peat bog destroyed by mining is like trying to restore an old growth forest. There are many factors to consider: Along with the mosses, the bogs support other plants and serve as a habitat for many types of birds, amphibians, insects, and mammals. Bogs prevent flooding by soaking up extra water, which they release slowly during times of drought. A drained and dry peat bog can actually catch fire and burn underground for years, emitting even more carbon!

ALTERNATIVES TO PEAT AS A SOIL CONDITIONER

If you need a soil amendment or conditioner, switch to sustainable products such as compost or aged manure, biochar (a charcoal-like substance made from burned organic material), cover crops, green manure, or leaf mold. If you need to loosen up your compost, mix in wood chips, which will aid water and nutrient absorption. (A small amount of gravel also works well.) Under almost any circumstances, quality compost will achieve better results than peat in terms of vigorous growth and greater numbers of flowers.

ALTERNATIVES TO PEAT FOR POTTING MIXES

Several different types of fibrous plant materials—including bark, coconut coir, grasses, hemp, paper, and wood fiber—are being studied for their effectiveness in potting mix and seed-starting mixtures.

A recent research paper determined well-shredded and composted pine bark (not pine nuggets, needles, or mulch) to perform as well as peat moss in seed germination trials.

Coir is a by-product of the coconut industry. Unlike acidic peat, it has a near-neutral pH and is easy to moisten from a dehydrated state. It soaks up seven times its dry weight in water and is very slow to decompose. Hydroponic growers have been using it for years.

POTTING SOIL SURROUNDED BY (LEFT TO RIGHT) RICE HULLS, VERMICULITE, PEAT, PERLITE, AND COCONUT COIR

SUNLIGHT AND WATER ESSENTIALS

A PLANT NEEDS TO DO MORE THAN STRETCH ITS LEAVES TOWARD THE SUN. IT ALSO NEEDS TO SEND DOWN ROOTS DEEP INTO THE GROUND. THEY HOLD ON TIGHTLY IN THE DARK, OUT OF SIGHT WHERE IT IS EASY TO FORGET ABOUT THEM. BUT IT IS THE FACT THAT A PLANT CAN DO THESE TWO THINGS AT ONCE, ANCHORING ITSELF TO THE EARTH EVEN AS IT REACHES FOR THE SKY, THAT MAKES IT STRONG.
–Cameron Dokey, American writer (b. 1956)

It's important to recognize and provide for every plant's needs—especially in terms of sunlight and water. Plants in a collection should be compatible in the container. In most cases—and most importantly—they should thrive in the same conditions and have not only similar sun and moisture requirements but also common nutrient needs.

LET IN THE SUNSHINE

All plants need the proper type and amount of sunlight. You must be mindful of the lighting where you will display your container. For example, does the spot get morning sun (which tends to be cooler), afternoon sun (which is usually hotter), or even partial shade (which could mean a period of shade during the hottest part of the afternoon and a period of sun in the morning or evening)?

If plants do not receive an adequate amount of sunlight, they will fail to thrive and bloom and eventually become lanky or stretched out and/or vulnerable to disease. This is why it is important that low-light plants be combined with other low-light plants and full-sun plants be planted with other full-sun plants—and so on, with almost every sun exposure in between. We say "almost" because sometimes you can push a plant's limits. A shade-loving plant may be paired with a sun-loving plant if the sun-lover's strongest exposure is in the morning and all receive adequate moisture, with more for the shade-lover if it appears stressed.

Having a good idea of the sunlight that will fall on your container will help you to choose compatible plants.

THE SUN'S DIFFERENT STROKES

■ **"Sun"** or **"full sun"** means that a plant requires at least 6 hours of direct sun every day. The sunlight need not be continuous sun as long as the total adds up to at least 6 hours. Full sun is best during midday; the low, slanting rays of sunlight in the early morning and evening are not full sun.

■ **"Partial sun"** and **"partial shade"** are often used interchangeably, but they are not the same.

"Partial sun" refers to the amount of sunlight received that is not full sun. Plants that require partial sun need 4 to 6 hours of direct sun each day and respond best to

A POTAGER GARDEN CONTAINING TOMATOES, HOT PEPPERS, AND PINEAPPLE SAGE

morning or early afternoon sunlight. These plants benefit from shade during intense afternoon heat.

"Partial shade" indicates that a plant needs less sunlight than "partial sun" but more than "shade"; specifically, this means 2 to 4 hours of direct sun per day. Partial shade plants need relief from the intense afternoon sun; suitable shade-throwers include a building wall, tree crown, or fence. (Do not simply cover a partial shade plant that is in the sun.) An eastern exposure for dappled sun is perfect.

■ **"Dappled sun"** is defined as filtered light, such as through tree branches and leaves. Some morning sun may also be suitable.

■ **"Shade"** or **"full shade"** describes fewer than 2 hours of direct sun per day, with filtered light during the rest of the day. It does not mean a dark, totally shaded location with no sunlight. Once established, plants that require full shade tend to be low-maintenance.

■ **"Shade"** can further be defined as follows:

"Light shade" describes partially filtered sun, such as conditions under open-canopied trees like honey

locust and birch, where there is an ever-moving pattern of sun and shade. Light shade may also be known as "dappled shade" or "intermittent shade."

"*Moderate shade*" refers to a spot where light is mostly reflected; one example is the floor of a hardwood forest.

"*Heavy shade*" or "*deep shade*" occurs when no direct sunlight reaches a spot, such as at the base of a north-facing wall or below dense tree cover.

THE WEIGHT OF WATER

Proper watering is essential. Almost every function performed by a plant involves water—seed-sprouting, photosynthesis, growth, and reproduction, among them—and up to 95% of a plant's tissue is water.

The frequency and amount of water required by container plants depends somewhat on the weather, the time of year, the location, the growing medium, the container size and material, and, of course, the plants. Some plants are heavy drinkers, some are light drinkers, and still others thrive in dry or semidry conditions. For the latter, too much water can be fatal.

In addition to knowing a plant's water requirements, observation is the key to watering enough and on time. Plants should be watered when they need moisture, not based on a general rule of thumb. There is one standard gauge: To know if a plant needs water, feel the soil by pressing a finger an inch or two into the soil. If it is dry, add water—enough to run out of the bottom of the pot.

By soaking the entire pot of soil, you will flush, or leach out, potentially damaging soluble salts that enter the container with "softened" water or fertilizer. Softened water is "hard" water that has been treated with sodium, but soluble salts can also appear naturally in water. An accumulation of salts can cause burned leaf margins (the result of salts being absorbed by the roots and moving up to the leaves) and damaged roots (if enough salts accumulate in the soil, the plant's water-absorbing root tips may be killed; soon thereafter, the plant may begin to wilt and drop leaves before eventually dying).

If you're not sure when to water plants in potting mix, look closely. This medium tends to pull away from the edges of its pot when it becomes excessively dry. Rewetting the medium may be a challenge, as water will tend to bypass it and flow out through the space between the medium and the pot. In order to rehydrate the medium, it is best to immerse the container in a sink or basin of water, allowing water to seep in through the holes, until the surface of the medium is moist again.

MORE WATER WAYS

• Plants should always be watered with an eye toward preventing severe wilting, which can affect the health and quality of a plant.

• Water frequently. Since containers don't benefit from ground moisture, it's important to water as often as once daily, if necessary. In hot, dry weather, you may need to water twice a day. This is especially true for closely spaced plants packed into a small volume of soil.

• Be sure to water all of the soil in the pot—not just around the edges. If you find that your containers are drying out too quickly, perhaps you have too much plant for the soil in the pot. If your plants are crowded, it might be time to repot them into a larger container. If they look past their prime, consider replacing them with new plants.

• Reduce watering in winter.

MY WATERING RECORD

PLANT	DATES WATERED AND EFFECTS

SWEET POTATO VINE, LANTANA, SUMMER SNAPRAGONS, AND EUPHORBIA

CARING FOR CONTAINER PLANTS

A GARDEN REQUIRES PATIENT LABOR AND ATTENTION. PLANTS DO NOT GROW MERELY TO SATISFY AMBITIONS OR TO FULFILL GOOD INTENTIONS. THEY THRIVE BECAUSE SOMEONE EXPENDED EFFORT ON THEM.

–Liberty Hyde Bailey, American horticulturist and botanist (1858–1954)

Pretty planters are wonderful as a welcome at the entrance to your home, as accent or focal pieces on the porch or patio, or as portable decor to place where you need a pop of color. However, containers do need to be maintained, and a little attention to details will go a long way toward the plants' success.

SPREAD MULCH

Mulch container surfaces to prevent soil compaction and/ or root damage. Heavy rains and high-pressure hose blasts can dislodge potting mix and damage roots or pound the surface and thus create a hard crust through which water has a difficult time penetrating.

Sphagnum moss, aquarium gravel, pebbles, and shredded cedar bark are all attractive barriers that thwart these problems. Cedar bark contains a resin that gives it the added advantage of giving off a pleasant aroma that repels many insects. The same effect can be achieved with cocoa bean mulch.

Note that it is important to keep bark mulch at least 2 inches away from stems.

DEADHEAD

"Deadheading" simply means removing spent blossoms. Regular deadheading encourages many plants to flower for longer. Pinch or cut off all of the old blossom—not just the petals—before it can set seeds. Try not to leave stumps. Cut back to above the first set of leaves below the faded flower, side bud, or side stem on the stalk where new blooms will form. "Leave" as much foliage as you can, as it is through this that the plant gets its energy.

Some flowers are "self-cleaning," meaning that they will push off their dead blossoms with no help from you. (Check to see if they have left a seedpod behind.) Here are some good reasons to keep up with deadheading . . .

■ **To prolong the bloom:** By not allowing your flowering plants to set seeds, you will allow them to keep producing more flowers. (A plant's mission is to ensure the survival of its species by making seeds that become the following year's plants. Once it has accomplished this task, the plant shuts down the "bloom factory.") Perennials have a well-defined season of bloom, but most annuals will keep producing blossoms until seeds form. By deadheading them, you will direct all of the energy needed to produce seeds right back into forming more flowers.

■ **To control self-sowers:** The purpose of self-sowing

plants is to set and spread seeds and take over Earth. To keep them under control, remove spent flowers before they can disperse their seeds. Common self-seeders include columbine, clustered bellflower, evening primrose, foxglove, mallow, phlox, and violets. Of course, if you want to scatter the seeds where you'd like them to grow, allow seeds to form at the end of their bloom season.

■ **To encourage reblooming:** Many perennials—including cardinal flower, centranthus, delphinium, foxglove, hollyhock, and tiarella—will produce a second flush of flowers later in the season if you remove the spent spring or early summer blossoms. When multiple flowers form on a single stalk, such as with hollyhocks or foxglove, you should carefully remove each spent blossom from the bottom up, while allowing the top buds to develop and bloom. When the stalk is finally spent, cut it off at the base but leave the foliage alone.

Hands off! Vegetable plants do not need deadheading. Any unpollinated or spent blooms will dry up and fall off.

PINCH

Pinching forces a plant to branch out, eventually growing bushier and producing more flowers of better quality. Clamp the tip of the plant stem between your thumb

and first finger and remove it by "pinching" it back to just above a leaf or bud. After the first heavy flush of blooms is spent, pinch again for another spectacular show. Impatiens and begonias especially benefit from an early pinch. (Pruning vining plants is also a form of pinching.) New shoots should develop along the stem to fill out the plant.

CLEAN UP

Remove plant debris from containers. If left, decaying leaves and blooms often foster diseases and invite insects.

PRUNE

Pruning is the act of removing leaves or branches to give shape to the plant, to eliminate those that are competing for space, or to remove damaged or diseased limbs or foliage. (When disease is suspected, disinfect tools; see "How to Clean Containers and Tools," page 16.) Prune trailing ("spiller") and climbing plants occasionally by as much as one-half of the stem to maintain the balance and aesthetics of your container. (Don't be surprised to see two or three vigorous new stems!)

Occasionally trim rambling plants—such as dichondras, ivies, licorice plants, and even petunias—to keep them from climbing over and smothering their neighbors. Pruning can and should be done throughout the summer.

FERTILIZING CONTAINER PLANTS

IF YOU WISH TO MAKE ANYTHING GROW, YOU MUST UNDERSTAND IT, AND UNDERSTAND IT IN A VERY REAL SENSE. "GREEN FINGERS" ARE A FACT, AND A MYSTERY ONLY TO THE UNPRACTICED. BUT GREEN FINGERS ARE THE EXTENSIONS OF A VERDANT HEART.

–Russell Page, English landscape architect (1906–85)

Whether you are growing ornamental or edible plants in containers, a continuous supply of nutrients is essential to their achievement of optimal performance and production levels; remember, existing nutrients are washed away every time you water. The type, timing, and amount of fertilizer that you use can make all the difference in the world—and overfertilizing any plant can damage it, even to the point of causing it to fail to thrive. (See "'FOOF': Fear of Overfertilizing," page 34.)

RELEASE ME!

Controlled-release and *slow-release* fertilizers are not the same. What's more, the names for them are not always the same.

Controlled-release fertilizers (CRFs) are also known as controlled availability fertilizers, delayed-release fertilizers, metered-release fertilizers, coated fertilizers, and slow-acting fertilizers—but for our purposes, we will call them simply "controlled-release fertilizers."

CRFs disperse their nutrients over a long period of time—much longer than that provided by uncoated, less-coated, or differently coated liquid fertilizers. Controlled-release longevities (the time that it takes to release all of the nutrients) range anywhere from 2 to 18 months. The longevity of controlled-release fertilizers is determined by the thickness of the semipermeable polymer/resin coating that surrounds the water-soluble fertilizer (the thicker the

coating, the slower the release) and the temperature of the soil, which should be around 72°F (indicated on packaging; the higher the temperature, the faster the release). The polymer/resin coating responds to ordinary rain- or tap water, and usually no additional liquid fertilizer is needed.

Note that treating annuals or perennials with a long-duration controlled-release fertilizer will not cause the plants to grow or perform beyond their normal seasonal life cycle.

Slow-release fertilizers (SRFs) also consist of water-soluble nutrients coated with a resin. These dispense their nutrients over less predictable time periods and under specific conditions related to their decomposition and soil bacterial activity, whose effectiveness is dependent on

FALSE BANANA COMBINED WITH DWARF WEEPING
LOROPETALUM AND CREEPING JENNY

cause nutrients to leach out. Application rates for liquid fertilizers can be altered to minimize nutrient loss: If a product advises using one scoop per gallon every 2 weeks, you can safely apply one-half scoop per gallon every week. In late summer, some plants may benefit from supplemental liquid fertilizer. However, in most cases, fertilization is not recommended after August to avoid delaying plant dormancy.

WELCOME WEEDS AND HERBS FOR DIY FERTILIZER

All-purpose, organic plant fertilizer can be made from just weeds and water. Common garden plants and even unwanted weeds hold vitamins and nutrients in their leaves that, as the leaves decompose, can be a quick source of macro- and micronutrients to feed the roots or leaves of fast-growing plants at the exact time that they need it.

The **N-P-K** fertilizer trio—**nitrogen, phosphorus, and potassium**—are the most important nutrients that a plant needs to thrive. Each of these can be found in specific plants; knowing how and when to use them will carry you through the season.

■ **Nitrogen** is needed for plants' vegetative growth. It should be used in the early stages of leaf and

soil temperature and moisture (release increases with higher temperatures and moisture). Slow-release fertilizers can be mixed into the medium at planting time or scratched into the soil surface in an amount that is based on the size of the container (consult the package).

WATER WORKERS

Uncoated **liquid fertilizers** provide plants with quick, easy access to nutrients that are delivered immediately upon application. Liquid fertilizers especially benefit plants in containers, where roots compete for space and frequent waterings

stem development and withheld later in the season when plants are flowering. Nitrogen-rich plants include comfrey, common mallow, and stinging nettle. Generally speaking, homemade brews tend to be less concentrated than commercial high-nitrogen fertilizers such as fish emulsion and are fine for use throughout the season.

■ **Phosphorus** is important at season's start for strong root growth, especially on developing root crops, new transplants, and tomato seedlings whose leaves have begun to turn purplish. Later, it helps plants to produce flowers and fruit. Add more chickweed, comfrey, lamb's-quarter, and stinging nettle to your brews at this time.

■ **Potassium** is needed for healthy roots and aids in fruit/flower growth. Potassium-rich weeds, which are great for boosting resilience to stress, include borage, chickweed, comfrey, dandelions, and lamb's-quarter.

Herbs such as **dried chamomile, oregano, sage,** and **dill** that have become old and unpalatable can also benefit DIY fertilizers, but note that these are slightly less nutrient-dense than weeds.

The quantities of specific nutrients found within each plant are not as precise as they are in a commercial fertilizer product. Every garden is different, and quantities are influenced by a host of factors.

What is important to understand is that all of the members of the unique and complex community of bacteria and other microbes,

VOICES OF EXPERIENCE

Container crops often need more help with resilience than those grown in-ground. I sometimes bury fresh shredded comfrey leaves halfway down into the container at the time of planting. The decaying plant matter provides a food source for growing plants as their root systems stretch deep into the pot.   –Gayla T., via Almanac.com

I use this three-step fertilizer program, and my container gardens flourish.

1. Fertilize when you are filling your containers with potting mix. If the potting mix contains fertilizer, skip this step. You want "slow-release" fertilizer pellets. Check the label for this information.

2. Fertilize as your plants grow. Apply a liquid fertilizer to supplement the slow-release fertilizer.

When buying liquid fertilizer, you want an equal ratio of "N-P-K." For tomatoes, peppers, and other fruiting plants, choose a liquid fertilizer with a higher K (potassium) number.

I water my vegetables with a diluted seaweed feed about once a month. Fruiting vegetables will need a tomato feed weekly (alternating with the seaweed feed once a month), from spring until late summer. Cut-and-come-again lettuces and other salad leaves don't typically need a regular feed. Herbs don't need to be fed at all—particularly lavender, rosemary, and thyme; they do best in nutrient-poor, drier conditions.

3. Fertilize if plants are stressed or need a pick-me-up. In this case, feed plant leaves directly (this is called "foliar feeding"). The spray delivers nutrients directly to where photosynthesis takes place. Results are dramatic—you'll see growth or renewal almost overnight. Don't foliar-feed when temperatures are above 90°F or when the Sun is beating down on plants directly. The fertilizer will burn leaves.

–Doreen H., via Almanac.com

A FRAGRANT MIX OF LAVENDER, MINT, ROSEMARY, AND SWEET LEAF

in the sun to allow the mixture to steep for at least a day.

■ Strain out and discard the weeds or herbs.

■ If necessary, dilute your finished fertilizer with water until it looks like weak tea.

■ Fill up a watering can or spray bottle with your fertilizer tea and then pour it into plant containers or spray the leaves of your plants with it so that it acts as a foliar (foliage) feed.

Note that the potency of fertilizer teas improves as the plants decompose. The best teas steep for days or even weeks. However, the high nitrogen content in some plants, such as comfrey and stinging nettle, eventually creates a slop that stinks! Save the most malodorous brews for outdoor use; apply mixes that have been brewed for no longer than a day or so to houseplants and seedlings grown indoors.

BREW BETTER

To make an even better brew, add an aquarium bubbler to your bucket as it steeps. Aeration during the brewing process helps to create a healthy, oxygenated fertilizer tea that is full of helpful bacteria and microorganisms. (It smells better, too.)

Stirring or agitating the mix by hand multiple times a day will achieve a similar effect, but a pump will do the work for you if you have an aerator.

invertebrates, and other life that your soil supports (aka the "soil food web") are involved in the processes of decomposition. How they interact with plant roots influences how effectively nutrients are made available.

THE BREW METHOD

The simplest method of making fertilizer is to brew the weeds and herbs, much as you would tea.

■ Stuff a bucket about half-full with roughly chopped leaves, stems, and flowers of weeds or pruned herbs. Pack them in tightly.

■ Fill the bucket with rain- or tap water. If desired, speed up the process by using heated (not boiling) water.

■ Cover the bucket with fine mesh to prevent mosquitoes from laying eggs in it. Set it aside

"FOOF": FEAR OF OVERFERTILIZING

EVERYTHING IN EXCESS IS OPPOSED TO NATURE.
–Hippocrates, Greek physician (c. 460–c. 370 B.C.)

You may have read that regular watering leaches, or washes out, existing fertilizer nutrients in a container. True enough, but this is no reason to fertilize more or more frequently; more is never better when it comes to fertilizer. Still, anybody can overdo it. Here are a few clues that you've added too much of a good thing to your container, with some advice about what to do next.

Excess fertilization can lead to high concentrations of soluble salts in your potting mix—and no good comes out of this. The salts can slow the dispersal of water to the roots and result in root disease and damping off.

It's likely that you have overdosed your container, if . . .
■ a crust of fertilizer forms on top of the planting medium
■ the lower leaves of plants turn yellow and wilt
■ the leaf tips and margins turn brown
■ plant roots are brown or black and limp

■ the plant loses leaves
■ plant growth is slow or nonexistent

It's not enough simply to know that you applied too much fertilizer. To avoid making the same mistake again, it's important to understand how and where you went wrong. The problem could be due to . . .
■ too much liquid fertilizer added at one time
■ several applications of fertilizer with little or no leaching (poor drainage)
■ too much slow-release fertilizer

■ use of controlled-release fertilizer with liquid fertilizer
■ insufficient moisture for the fertilization rate

What to do now? Leach problem plants and, in the future, use fertilizer products wisely:
■ When a liquid fertilizer is the source of the excess salts, apply tap water (about twice as much as the volume of the container) and allow it to run out of the bottom of the container; repeat in 2 to 3 hours or the next day.
■ Stick with one type of fertilizer.
■ Read product labels to learn the proper proportions/ amounts of fertilizers.
■ When moving plants to a slow-growth environment (e.g., putting them in a basement or garage to overwinter), leach excess fertilizer from the medium.
■ Calculate the proper amount of liquid fertilizer and mix it with enough water to ensure that 10% of it will wash out of the container's bottom.

MY FERTILIZER RECORD

DATE	PLANT	FERTILIZER	NOTES

BALCONY, TERRACE, AND ROOFTOP GARDENING IN CONTAINERS

I'VE JUST GOT A FLAT WITH A LITTLE BALCONY, SO I DID THAT FANTASTIC THING OF BUYING FAR TOO MANY PLANTS AND NOT REALLY KNOWING WHAT WAS GOING TO STAY ALIVE AND WHAT WASN'T.
–Natasia Demetriou, English comedienne and actress (b. 1984)

How do you garden in an apartment or con-do without a proper yard? Grow in containers on a balcony, rooftop, terrace, or patio! If conditions are right, vegetables, fruit, herbs, flowers, and more will flourish in containers. Before you go out to buy plants, read on.

1. Check the rules for your building. Some buildings don't allow any plants on balconies or allow only flowers (as vegetables may attract birds or pests).

2. At the same time, inquire about the weight-bearing capacity of your balcony or rooftop. Terra-cotta and ceramic pots are heavy, so you might need to use rice pots, plastic or fiberglass containers, or fabric grow bags combined with lightweight potting mixes.
■ Plan to arrange beds and larger containers around the outside edges of a balcony to define the space and spread out the load. Make use of wall space to hang half-baskets and wall pockets or a hook for a hanging basket.

3. Think through how you'll manage the watering chores. Plants in containers need to be watered often. If you are growing on a rooftop, consider how far you will be lugging jugs of water. You might want to look into drip irrigation or self-watering pots (see "Make a Self-Watering Container," page 14). You can also invest in a watering can that is easy to fill from the bathtub. Take care that excess water from your plants doesn't rain down on neighbors below. Be courteous and put saucers or trays under your plants to collect the overflow.

4. If you're a beginner, **start small with a few pots.** You can always add more. You need to get a sense of how much time you have to maintain and care for your garden. You'll be discouraged if you overdo it.

5. **Plan for success.** Choosing the right plants for your site is most important. Don't waste space on something that is not going to thrive.

The amount of sunlight is the most critical question:

■ *Does your balcony face south and receive direct sun all day long?* Cacti, many flowers, and most vegetables—if kept well watered—will love it there.

■ *Does your balcony face north, or is it shaded by other buildings for most of the day?* If so, look to low-light plants. Among flowers, these would include begonias, coleuses, ferns, hostas, and impatiens. If you want to grow edibles, you might try greens like chard, spinach, or lettuce, which can grow with less than a half day of sun. Some culinary herbs manage, too.

■ *It's easy to overestimate the amount of sunlight you get.* Remember that the length of day and Sun's angle change daily. Keep in mind that most veggies need a minimum of 6 to 8 hours of sun per day to grow well and produce.

6. **Consider other weather effects on your balcony or rooftop.** Is your space windy? The higher up you are, the more wind you are likely to experience, and hot, dry winds can quickly parch your plants. Intense heat with no wind can also be an issue. Look into self-watering pots (see page 14) or be prepared to water more frequently. To temper the wind, install a lattice or wire trellis as a wind block, which will support your climbing vines as well as provide a bit of privacy.

VOICE OF EXPERIENCE

I had full western exposure on an old brick building and it got toasty! Generally, my strategy was to have a couple of tall pots with very tough plants in them and then nestle smaller things into their (still bright) shade to help to keep them cooler.

I've never had such happy hot peppers as when I was balcony-growing! If you like hot peppers, give them a try on your balcony.

Try to think of everything: Frost, high winds, building inspections, moving, construction in the balcony above yours that sends down dust and debris—your life will be easier if you set up your pots in such a way that everything can come inside relatively quickly.

Get yourself a heavy watering can, if possible. To keep my plastic one from blowing around, I had to put a big chunk of brick in it when I was done watering and wedge it behind the pots. This was frugal but annoying.

Don't forget scent! If you don't have a lot of space for blooms, you can still pack a lot of different scents into your space. I found the different scented thymes, lemon verbena, rose-scented geraniums, and mint to be well suited to baking heat and small space.

There's always a way. If you want a grapevine, you can have a grapevine! Trellising designed to be sunk into the ground can be planted in pots; you just need one or two anchor points at the top or, lacking that, a little quick-set concrete and the sacrifice of a few garden pots to the cause to make the base extra stable. –*Kate, via Almanac.com*

SOME ENLIGHTENMENT ABOUT GROW LIGHTS

COME FORTH INTO THE LIGHT OF THINGS, LET NATURE BE YOUR TEACHER.
–William Wordsworth, English poet (1770–1850)

Indoor gardening enables you to start seeds or have fresh edibles throughout the dormant days of winter until it's time to grow outdoors—or even year-round, especially if outdoor gardening is not an option. Indoor techniques and technology abound, from elaborate hydroponic systems to expensive mini-greenhouses and more. One need that they all share is lighting. If you're in the dark about this, read on.

THE SPECTRUM

Grow-light options are wide-ranging, from fluorescent to HID (high-intensity discharge) to LED (light-emitting diode). Each type has an array of power requirements, brightness levels, and color temperatures.

■ **Compact Fluorescent Lamp (CFL) Lights,** aka common household fluorescents, are an effective supplement to natural (window) light. When starting seeds, use a "full-spectrum" fluorescent bulb made specifically for fruiting or flowering plants. For best results, place the bulb in a directional lamp 3 to 6 inches above the plant(s).

■ **High-Intensity Discharge (HID) Lights** are ideal for growing maturing edible plants. However, HIDs need to be replaced more frequently, are expensive, use electricity inefficiently, and give off heat. Despite this, they are widely used in plant nurseries and large-scale grow houses because of their raw power.

■ **Light-Emitting Diode (LED) Lights:** For efficiently growing large numbers of plants, full-spectrum LEDs provide the best results. They use significantly less power to produce more light than traditional CFLs, and they produce very little heat. Although LEDs are more expensive than fluorescent bulbs, the LED lifetime is far longer.

THE SPECS

Before you purchase grow lights, decide how many plants you want to illuminate and how much area they will occupy under the light(s). This will enable you to calculate how many lightbulbs you'll need.

Think about how to position the light(s) over the plants so that you can easily alter the distance between the lights and the plants as they grow. Common options include suspending the lights from chains above your plants (e.g., on the ceiling or a sawhorse) and adjusting the chains as the plants grow. Or, stabilizing the light(s) and setting the planters on a stack of books, removing volumes as needed to lower the maturing plants.

Remember, too, that each type of grow light provides a different amount of light. To be most effective, each light should be a specific distance from the plants: Fluorescent lights should be no more than 12 inches above the tops of the plants; HIDs, 24 to 60 inches; and LEDs, 12 to 24 inches.

The distance between the tops of plants and lighting will vary based on the wattage of lights and the stage of growth. Check plants regularly for signs of heat stress (light too close) or legginess (not enough light); adjust the position of lighting as needed.

Plants grown under lights indoors need more hours of light than the same plants do outdoors. Grow lights should be on for at least 14 but no more than 18 hours per day; even indoor plants need a minimum of 6 hours of darkness each day.

OBSERVATIONS AND REMINDERS

ABOUT MY CONTAINER GARDEN

OBSERVATIONS AND REMINDERS

CHANGES TO MAKE NEXT YEAR

Make life—and gardening—easy with *The Old Farmer's Almanac* Garden Planner
software, a powerful yet simple tool with access to info on hundreds of plants.
Activate your free 7-day trial at GardenPlanner.Almanac.com.

EDIBLES

SALAD GREENS AND
HERBS PAIR BEAUTIFULLY
TOGETHER.

SECRETS TO GROWING FOOD IN CONTAINERS

LIFE BEGINS THE DAY YOU START A GARDEN.
–Chinese proverb

Almost any "standard-size" vegetable that you can grow in the ground can be cultivated in a container if the conditions—for example, soil, sun, space, and water—are right. Here are some tips and suggestions for making the most of the "standards" in your potted garden:

■ **To keep plants adequately cool and moist, double-pot them** by placing a small pot inside a larger one and filling the space between them with sphagnum moss or crumpled newspaper. When watering the plant, also soak the filler between the pots. The moist filler acts as insulation. Make sure that both containers have drainage holes to prevent standing water.

■ For proper growth, **vegetables need consistently moist soil.** Wind and warmth draw moisture from plant leaves, drying them out, so many plants must be watered as often as twice a day. To save work, use self-watering containers, which have a water reservoir in the bottom to transfer water to the dry soil as needed. (See "Make a Self-Watering Container," page 14.)

■ When setting seeds, **follow the spacing guidelines on the seed packet.** Plant slightly closer only if you are able to maintain a strict water and fertilizing schedule and monitor the plants for disease (close planting reduces air circulation and increases the risk of disease).

■ You can **grow vegetables and compatible flowers together**—adding both color and function—but don't plant them too close to one another, as they will compete for light.

■ To maximize space and thus your harvest, **plant root crops, low growers, and tall climbers together** in the same container.

■ **Mix quick-maturing plants,** such as lettuce or radishes, **with longer-growing ones,** like tomatoes or broccoli.

■ **Group plants with similar needs for sun and water,** such as lettuce, pole beans, and radishes; beets, bush beans, and cucumbers; basil, onions, and tomatoes; and bok choy, carrots, and peas.

■ **Think pretty as well as practical.** For example, the vigorous vines of Italian heirloom 'Trionfo Violetto' pole beans are covered with dark green, purple-vein leaves, and their lavender flowers give rise to dark purple pods.

■ For climbing varieties, **put trellises, stakes, or other** supports in place at planting time; stakes inserted into containers later in the season may injure the plant's roots. If a trellis becomes top-heavy, it may need to be attached to something other than the pot to prevent it from tipping over. Position the container near a fence, wall, or deck railing for additional support.

■ "Intercropping" means growing two or more crops together to save space. Set plants close enough that their leaves will touch, shading the soil between them when they are fully mature. This will keep weeds down and conserve moisture.

■ Some intercropping partners thrive if their roots occupy a different depth of soil. Pairing shallow-root vegetables, such as bush beans, with deeply rooted beets makes good use of space without creating root competition. Similarly, planting heavy feeders such as cabbage or cucumbers with light-feeding beans or carrots reduces the competition for soil nutrients.

CONTAINER CAVEATS

While almost any vegetable can be grown in a container, there are some exceptions. Before you invest time, money, and effort, consider this:

■ Sweet corn requires a substantial amount of space for numerous plants to ensure sufficient pollination. Containers

CONTAINER CAPACITIES

SIZE	DIAMETER/ WIDTH (INCHES)	HEIGHT (INCHES)	VOLUME	SUGGESTED PLANTS
1-gallon	8 to 14	5 to 7	4 quarts	Asian greens (under 12 inches), lettuce (dwarf heads), seedlings/transplants
2-gallon	9½ to 14	6 to 9	8 quarts	Asian greens (up to 20 inches), baby beets, carrots (short), lettuce (dwarf heads)
3-gallon	11 to 21	6 to 12	12 quarts	Asian greens (up to 20 inches), beets, bok choy, carrots (short), chard (Swiss), endive, herbs (all), lettuce, mesclun, radishes, spinach, tomatoes (micro-dwarf), turnips
4-gallon	11 to 25	6 to 12	16 quarts (½ bushel)	Asian greens (all), beans (bush, fava, soy), chard (Swiss), endive, beets, carrots (short), herbs (all), mesclun, radishes, spinach, tomatoes (dwarf up to 4 feet), turnips
5-gallon	12 to 14	9½ to 14	20 quarts	Asian greens (all), beans (bush or pole), beets, broccoli, brussels sprouts, cabbage, carrots (all), cauliflower, celery, chard (Swiss), collards, endive, herbs (all), kale, mesclun, muskmelon (cantaloupe), peas, peppers, potatoes (including sweet), radishes, squash (winter and summer), spinach, tomatoes (all dwarf), turnips, watermelons
6- to 8-gallon	12 to 24	8 to 15	24 to 32 qts. (¾ to 1 bushel)	Brussels sprouts, muskmelon (cantaloupe), potatoes (including sweet), squash (winter and summer), tomatoes (beefsteak/large determinate), watermelons
9- to 12-gallon	16 to 19	11½ to 15	36 to 48 quarts	Brussels sprouts, muskmelon (cantaloupe), potatoes (including sweet), squash (winter and summer), tomatoes (beefsteak/large determinate), watermelons, or a mix of multiple items

are not a practical means.

■ Some standard vining plants—**melons, pumpkins, and squashes**—**find insufficient room to roam** in even the largest containers. Choose bush-type cultivars whenever possible.

■ **Determinate tomato cultivars,** which are bred to grow to a certain height and require little support, **are better suited to containers** than indeterminate types, which tend to sprawl and require a cage or other support.

SUGGESTED SOIL DEPTHS

Actual need may vary, depending on plant variety . . .

■ For **shallow-root vegetables** (chives, green onions, lettuces, radishes, spinach): 6 to 9 inches

■ For **moderate-depth vegetables** (beans, beets, broccoli, short varieties of carrots, cauliflower, celery, chard, eggplant, kale, peas, peppers): 12 to 18 inches

■ For **deep-root vegetables** (cucumbers, potatoes, tomatoes, winter and summer squashes): 18 to 24 inches

With good timing and careful planning, you can harvest tiny vegetables from full-size plants if you pick when they're petite. Many "baby" vegetables are grown on standard plants and harvested while they are still tiny. Baby beets, served greens and all, or petite summer squash picked with the flower still attached are ideal for eating long before they reach maturity.

VOICES OF EXPERIENCE

I have learned two things with container gardening over the past 2 years: (1) drainage holes are necessary, or your plants may drown in weekly downpours, and (2) on account of the drainage holes, you will need to water your plants daily. So, if you are going on vacation, call a neighbor or you will come home to some sun-dried tomatoes.

–*LoriLovesPink, via Almanac.com*

There are lots of other types of summer squash, besides zucchini, that grow more bushlike. Pattypans (scallop), yellow crookneck, and yellow straight neck squashes can be grown in pots. Eggplants grown in pots do quite well. Of course, hot peppers, especially the ornamental ones, do well, too. Some look beautiful as hanging plants because the stems flow over the side of the pots. Determinate tomatoes (the ones that grow like little bushes) are great for pots, although by using a 5-gallon bucket and providing support, you can easily grow indeterminate varieties (the vining type). The same applies for pole beans. Also, there are bush-type cucumbers to be grown in pots. Stick a few garlic cloves in one or grow some cutting celery in some, along with many other herbs like basil, tarragon (buy French, as Russian loses its flavor on older plants), oregano, stevia, mint, and so forth. In the fall, you can grow collards, kale, broccoli, and so on. These are all the types of things that I grow in pots very successfully.

–*turtlewoman797, via Almanac.com*

Most all of my planting has been in containers. I even recovered and planted a potato that vined in the compost bin in an old cooler and got great potatoes later. –*Leigh, via Almanac.com*

I have been growing all types of tomatoes, cucumbers, peppers, eggplants, brussels sprouts, broccoli, and herbs in 5-gallon buckets and other containers for years. As long as they have been cleaned and have good drainage, you can use anything. One year, I even used a wicker basket that I put a trash bag in and filled with soil (poked holes for drainage).

–*Shari, via Almanac.com*

MY CONTAINER VEGGIES

PLANT	PLANTING DATE	OBSERVATIONS

BEANS

Phaseolus spp.

**BEANS ARE SUCH A NICE, NEUTRAL CANVAS:
YOU CAN MAKE A BIG, BASIC POT OF THEM AND THEN PLAY
AROUND WITH THEM DIFFERENTLY EVERY DAY.**
–*Crescent Dragonwagon, American writer (b. 1952)*

Y ou can't beat beans! Beans are one of the easiest vegetables to grow. The hard part may be deciding which ones to plant—some 40,000 varieties are believed to exist.

The focus here is on bush and pole, or vining, beans and ideally on compact or dwarf varieties. Bush beans tend to be compact plants, standing about 2 feet tall and seldom needing support. Pole beans produce vines that can reach to 10 or more feet and need a trellis or other support to climb. They require more attention than bush beans but tend to produce a bigger harvest because they are so much larger. To increase a bush bean harvest and extend the season, start an additional container 10 to 14 days after the first.

PLANTING

Prepare a container: An 8-inch-deep, 8-inch-wide container will hold one bush plant, while a 5-gallon pot will hold up to three bush or pole plants. For pole beans, plan to provide support in or immediately outside of the container.

Fill the container with potting mix and rich compost.

Beans grow best when direct-seeded (not transplanted) into the soil, whether it's in a container or the ground. After all danger of frost has passed, sow into warm (55°F or higher), moist soil. Put two beans into each hole between 1 and 1½ inches deep. Eliminate the weaker one after germination by cutting the stem. (Do not allow two plants to coexist in one hole; neither will thrive.)

RECOMMENDED VARIETIES

Many compact varieties are available, and many standard beans can be grown in containers as well.

Bush

• *Phaseolus lunatus* 'White Dixie Butterpea': 16 to 24 inches tall; three to four small lima beans per pod; excellent for hot weather climates

• *P. vulgaris* 'Derby': tender, round, 7-inch-long pods form on 18-inch plants; resistant to bean common mosaic virus

• *P. vulgaris* 'Mascotte': prolific producer; 5- to 6-inch fruit on 16- to 18-inch-tall plants; resistant to anthracnose, bean common mosaic virus, and halo blight; variety name is French for "mascot" and symbolizes good luck

• *P. vulgaris* 'Topcrop': vigorous heirloom that sets heavy crop of pods 6 to 7 inches long on 15- to 18-inch-tall bushes; resistant to bean common mosaic virus

Pole

• *P. coccineus* 'Hestia': dwarf runner bean; 12- to 14-inch-tall plants produce 8-inch-long pods; if desired, leave beans to dry on plant and harvest as dried beans for chili, soups, and stews

• *P. vulgaris* 'Rattlesnake': heirloom; vines up to 10 feet long produce 8- to 10-inch-long green pods with purple speckles; drought-resistant; heat-tolerant

FOR POLE BEANS, PLAN TO PROVIDE SUPPORT IN OR IMMEDIATELY OUTSIDE OF THE CONTAINER.

CARE

Provide 6 to 8 hours of sun per day.

Whenever the soil is dry, water to a depth of 1 to 2 inches.

Fertilize with a low-nitrogen formula (5-10-10) diluted to half-strength to avoid excess foliage growth. Apply at planting time and when plants begin to flower.

DISEASES/PESTS *(see pages 184–200)*

Although container bean plants—often being in a compact space and rather isolated from other plantings—are usually less susceptible to diseases and pests than those planted in-ground, here we include many that may affect beans, regardless of how planted.

Diseases: anthracnose, halo blight, powdery mildew, rust, Sclerotinia white mold, viruses (including bean common mosaic virus). *Pests:* aphids, cabbage loopers, corn earworms (aka tomato fruitworms), cucumber beetles, cutworms, Japanese beetles, leafhoppers, Mexican bean beetles, root-knot nematodes, slugs/snails, stinkbugs, whiteflies, wireworms.

HARVEST/STORAGE

■ Harvest frequently to keep plants producing well.

■ Snap or cut beans off stems, being careful not to tear the plants.

■ Refrigerate fresh beans in a plastic bag for up to 5 days or trim, blanch, and freeze them.

WIT & WISDOM

● *"String" beans have a fibrous, sometimes tough, thread running the length of their pod that for centuries had to be removed by hand. In the late 1800s, breeders became successful in eliminating the string in most varieties; today, only heirloom beans still have string.*

● *"Green" beans, "snap" beans, and "string" beans are all the same.*

● *Not all green beans are in fact green. Their colors can range from purple to red to yellow to streaked variations thereof.*

CARROTS

Daucus carota

IF YOU TRULY GET IN TOUCH WITH A PIECE OF CARROT,
YOU GET IN TOUCH WITH THE SOIL, THE RAIN, THE SUNSHINE.
YOU GET IN TOUCH WITH MOTHER EARTH AND EATING
IN SUCH A WAY, YOU FEEL IN TOUCH WITH TRUE LIFE, YOUR
ROOTS, AND THAT IS MEDITATION.

–Thich Nhat Hanh, Vietnamese Zen master (1926–2022)

Get in touch with a whole carrot: Grow your own! Carrots are a versatile vegetable that can be a bit tricky to grow but not so tricky that they can not be mastered. After all, they have a long history, dating from 3000 B.C. The orange-color carrot is relatively new to gardens and kitchens: It first appeared in the Netherlands in the 17th century. Carrots did not become popular in the United States until after World War I, when soldiers returning from Europe brought seeds and stories of having eaten and enjoyed them.

Today, carrots in every color are a good source of vitamins, nutrients, and fiber. To grow them is to know them!

PLANTING

It is important to grow carrots in a container that is deep enough for them at maturity. For baby or dwarf carrots, a 6- to 8-inch-deep container is needed. Standard carrots need a depth of at least 12 inches, if necessary, to accommodate a particular variety's length.

Carrots are a cool-season crop usually grown in the spring; seeds can be sown 2 to 3 weeks before the last spring frost.

Prepare a loose, well-draining potting mix with a portion of compost or organic matter. Add a handful of bonemeal; it contains phosphorus, which benefits root crops. Also add low-nitrogen fertilizer, per the package directions based on the container size. Water the soil evenly to moisten.

Sow the seeds about a ½ inch apart and ¼ inch deep. (Carrot seeds are tiny and thus difficult to drop individually; pelleted seeds or seed-taped ones are good alternative means.) Cover with a very light

RECOMMENDED VARIETIES

• *Daucus carota var. sativus* 'Adelaide': true baby carrot; miniature Nantes type (cylindrical, smooth, nearly same diameter from end to end; blunt, not pointed tip); mature at 3 to 4 inches

• *D. carota var. sativus* 'Bambino': harvest at 4 inches; dwarf tops; cylindrical, blunt roots; good for canning and pickling

• *D. carota var. sativus* 'Little Finger': heirloom; miniature Nantes type; 3 to 4 inches long; good for canning and pickling

• *D. carota var. sativus* 'Romance': Nantes type; 6 to 7 inches long, with tapered root; orange roots brighten after washing

• *D. carota var. sativus* 'Romeo': 1- to 1½-inch rounds; smooth skin, needs no peeling

• *D. carota var. sativus* 'Thumbelina': heirloom; 1- to 2-inch rounds; needs no peeling

• *D. carota var. sativus* 'Touchon': heirloom; considered best of the Nantes type; quick to mature; 6 inches long

WIT & WISDOM

- *Wild carrot, aka Queen Anne's lace, is native to Europe and Asia and an invasive species in North America. Its long taproots smell like carrots.*
- *Feathery green carrot tops were once used to decorate women's hats and sleeves.*

sprinkling of soil. Water gently (a handheld pump container is advised instead of a hose, the water force from which can displace the cover soil and seeds).

CARE

Water regularly to keep the soil moist. Container soils tend to dry relatively quickly. Dry soil can promote forking (misshapen roots).

When carrot tops are 2 to 3 inches tall, thin them to 1½ to 3 inches apart, based on the carrot size at maturity. Use scissors to cut off the tops, rather than pulling seedlings and disturbing the roots.

Apply a low-nitrogen fertilizer every 3 to 4 weeks, per the package directions for the size of the container.

DISEASES/PESTS *(see pages 184–200)*

Although container carrots—often being in a compact space and rather isolated from other plantings—are usually less susceptible to diseases and pests than those planted in-ground, here we include many that affect almost all carrots, regardless of how planted.

Diseases: aster yellows, bacterial leaf spot (or blight), black (Itersonilia) canker, fungal leaf spot (including Alternaria and Cercospora leaf blights), powdery mildew, Sclerotinia white mold. *Pests:* aphids, carrot rust flies, cutworms, flea beetles, root-knot nematodes, whiteflies, wireworms.

HARVEST/STORAGE

Check your seed packet for days to maturity or pull one to check its size. Carrots continue to grow, so harvest only as many as needed. Pull every second or third one to minimize disturbances to the plants.

Store carrots without their tops: Cut off all but ½ inch of the greens. Wash the carrots gently with cold water and then air-dry before refrigerating them in plastic bags. (Failing to do this and simply putting them into the refrigerator will cause them to go limp.)

CARROTS ARE A COOL-SEASON CROP
USUALLY GROWN IN THE SPRING.

CUCUMBERS

Cucumis sativus

O, FOR A LODGE IN A GARDEN OF CUCUMBERS!
–Rossiter Johnson, American writer (1840–1931)

Lacking a lodge? Cucumbers can be happy on the patio, porch, or balcony in a container.

Bush types are relatively small, compact plants that do well in pots, yet their fruit—in many cases—are as large as those produced on vines. At the same time, don't rule out vining cucumbers. Although these need to climb a trellis or cage, you can usually place such support in the container or immediately outside it.

Scientifically speaking, the cucumber is a member of the Cucurbitaceae family, making it a cousin to gourds, squashes, and some melons. Practically speaking, it is a popular, prolific, and easy-to-grow vegetable, high in water content (about 95%), low in calories (about 8 in a serving), and a good source of fiber and vitamins (specifically, K and A).

PLANTING

Cucumbers need a pot that is at least 12 inches wide. If a trellis or other support is needed, place it in or next to the pot prior to planting. Anchor it securely and gently tie plants to it as they grow.

No earlier than 2 weeks before the last spring frost, or when the soil has reached 70°F, sow two seeds about 1 inch deep in moistened potting mix. (Warm soil temperature is also recommended if transplanting seedlings.)

Water when seedlings emerge.

RECOMMENDED VARIETIES

Bush

• *Cucumis sativus* 'Bush Champion': compact, 8- to 10-inch-tall plants produce 8- to 12-inch fruit; 24-inch spread; resistant to cucumber mosaic virus

• *C. sativus* 'H-19 Little Leaf': compact, multibranching plant produces 3- to 5-inch fruit; needs no pollination; resistant to angular leaf spot, anthracnose, bacterial wilt, downy mildew, and scab; good pickler

• *C. sativus* 'Parisian Gherkin': small, 10- to 12-inch-tall plants produce 2- to 4-inch fruit; semi-vining form; resistant to cucumber mosaic virus and scab; good pickler

• *C. sativus* 'Salad Bush': compact, 6- to 8-inch-tall plant; early producer of 8-inch fruit; 26-inch spread; resistant to cucumber mosaic virus, powdery mildew, and scab

Vining

• *C. sativus* 'Picklebush': compact, 2-foot-long vines produce 4- to 5-inch fruit; resistant to cucumber mosaic virus and powdery mildew; good pickler

• *C. sativus* 'Spacemaster 80': 2- to 3-foot-long vines produce 7$\frac{1}{2}$-inch-long fruit (can drape over a container or attach to a trellis); resistant to cucumber mosaic virus, downy mildew, powdery mildew, and scab

WIT & WISDOM

- *A favorite vegetable for more than 3,000 years, the cucumber originated in northern India and was cultivated in China before spreading to Europe and points beyond.*

- *The name for the cucumber evolved from Europeans. To Romans, it was known as* cucumerem; *the French call(ed) it* concombre; *the English, who at first saw its value only as animal feed, referred to it as "cowcumber."*

PICK REGULARLY TO AVOID BITTER-TASTING CUCUMBERS.

CARE

Provide 6 to 8 hours of sun per day.

Remove the weaker seedling following germination (cut the weak one's stem at soil level rather than pulling it out; this is less disturbing to the roots).

Water regularly to keep soil moist but avoid wetting the leaves. (Consider watering from the bottom by putting the pot on a saucer or other vessel and adding water to it as needed.)

After the first true leaves appear, apply a slow-release pellet fertilizer based on the package directions for the pot size. Follow with low-nitrogen, high-potassium fertilizer every 10 to 14 days. (Too much nitrogen may cause a plant to produce more leaves than flowers and/or cause flowers to fail.)

Protect from cucumber beetles with a row cover, if desired, until flowers appear—then remove it to allow for pollination.

DISEASES/PESTS *(see pages 184–200)*

Although container cucumber plants—often being in a compact space and rather isolated from other plantings—are usually less susceptible to diseases and pests than those planted in-ground, here we include many that affect all cucumbers, regardless of how planted.

Diseases: angular leaf spot, anthracnose, bacterial wilt, blossom-end rot, downy mildew, Phytophthora crown and root rot, powdery mildew, scab, Sclerotinia white mold, viruses (including cucumber mosaic virus). *Pests:* aphids, corn earworms (aka tomato fruitworms), cucumber beetles, cutworms, spider mites, squash bugs, whiteflies.

HARVEST/STORAGE

Pick regularly; failure to do so can reduce production or lead to hard-skin, bitter-tasting fruit.

Use a knife or pruners to remove; pulling fruit off the vine may damage the vine.

Before storing, wash thoroughly with cool water and remove any debris. Allow to dry completely, then place in perforated plastic bags. Cucumbers will keep in the refrigerator for 7 to 10 days.

EGGPLANTS

Solanum melongena

Ah, the auspicious aubergine! Good luck comes to those who dream of the eggplant (called the *aubergine* in French). Good harvests come to those who grow it. This member of the nightshade family—and cousin to tomatoes and peppers—shares their preference for warm temperatures (near 70°F at night; higher in daytime), rich soil, consistent watering, and abundant sunshine. There are dozens of types of eggplants, many shapes, and several colors. Here we identify a few that are well suited to containers.

PLANTING

Prepare one 5-gallon container per 3-plus-foot-tall plant or a 2-gallon pot for dwarf/miniatures up to 2 feet tall with potting mix and compost or organic matter, as well as a slow-release fertilizer.

Eggplants are a warm-season crop. Start seeds indoors 6 to 8 weeks before the last frost date or purchase seedlings.

Plant outside when evening temperatures are consistently at least 65°F. If no compost or organic matter is added to the potting mix, fertilize seedlings with a (low-nitrogen) 5-10-10 formula.

Provide support (a tomato cage or wooden stake, with soft ties) for larger plants.

CARE

Provide 6 to 8 hours of sun per day.

Water consistently but not constantly; allow the plant to dry somewhat between waterings (inconsistent watering may result in irregular fruit shapes).

When fruit appear, begin using a

10-10-10 formula every 10 to 14 days.

Protect from temperatures below 55°F with cover or by moving.

DISEASES/PESTS *(see pages 184–200)* Although container eggplants—often being in a compact space and rather isolated from other plantings—are usually less susceptible to diseases and pests than those planted in-ground, here we include many that affect all eggplants, regardless of how planted.

Diseases: blossom-end rot, damping off, early blight, fungal leaf spot (especially Cercospora), Phytophthora crown and root rot, powdery mildew, southern bacterial wilt, Verticillium wilt. *Pests:* Colorado potato beetles, flea beetles, spider mites, tomato hornworms, whiteflies.

HARVEST/STORAGE
Pick regularly to encourage continued production. The fruit should have glossy skin and a firm body. As a rule, it is better to harvest eggplant just before it is ripe than to wait too long.

To avoid stem damage, use a sharp knife or pruning shears to cut the fruit from the plant.

Eggplant is best when used fresh, but it can be stored in the refrigerator. Wash, dry, place in a perforated plastic bag, and store in the crisper for up to 5 days. To freeze, wash, peel, and slice or cube the flesh; blanch or steam it for 4 minutes. Set eggplant on paper towels to drain and cool, then place in zip-close bags.

RECOMMENDED VARIETIES

- *Solanum melongena* var. *esculentum* 'Black Beauty': compact, 18- to 24-inch-tall plant produces dark purple-black, egg-shape fruit, 4 to 6 inches in diameter; harvest young, as age brings seediness

- *S. melongena* var. *esculentum* 'Fairy Tale': compact, 18- to 24-inch-tall plant; early producer of clusters of 4-inch-long, slender, lavender-and-white–striped fruit

- *S. melongena* var. *esculentum* 'Gretel': 24- to 36-inch-tall plant produces 3- to 4-inch-long, slender white fruit with tender skin, few seeds, and sweet flavor

- *S. melongena* var. *esculentum* 'Hansel': 24- to 36-inch-tall plant produces 3- to 10-inch-long fruit; prized for its slender purple fruit, few seeds, and sweet flavor

- *S. melongena* var. *esculentum* 'Patio Baby': miniature, 16- to 20-inch-tall plant produces 2- to 3-inch-long purple fruit; good choice for shorter growing seasons

WIT & WISDOM

- *Believed to have originated in India, eggplant was introduced to the United States by ever-curious President Thomas Jefferson in 1806 after he had been given one by a friend in France.*

- *In 5th-century China, fashionable women used a black dye made from eggplant skin to stain their teeth—which, when then polished, shined like metal.*

ONIONS

Allium cepa

IT IS HARD TO IMAGINE A CIVILIZATION WITHOUT ONIONS.
–Julia Child, American culinary expert (1912–2004)

WIT & WISDOM

● *Onions were worshiped in ancient Egypt, where their concentric circles were seen as symbols of eternal life.*

● *Onion's skin very thin, / Mild winter coming in. / Onion's skin thick and tough, / Coming winter cold and rough.* –Gardener's rhyme

---

If you're going to grow onions, consider their many layers. Onions are frost-hardy biennials grown as annuals. Cool weather produces green tops (leaves), while warm weather—ideally, 75°F—produces bulbs.

Onions can be grown from seeds, sets, and plants.

■ **Onion seeds** need to be started very early indoors. Seeds are both more widely available and less expensive than sets or plants.

■ **Onion sets** are onion bulbs that are ready to be planted in the spring. These were started as seeds, grew for a season, and then were uprooted and overwintered in storage. They are easy to plant and will produce full-size onions, but the choice of varieties is limited.

■ **Onion plants** (transplants) are limited in availability and choice, depending on your local garden center and mail-order vendors. They must be planted immediately.

Onions are "photoperiodic," which means that they grow in response to day length—the number of daylight hours needed to trigger bulb formation.

■ **Short-day onions** grow best in the southern United States, between 25° and 35° north latitude, and start bulbs when day length reaches 10 to 12 hours. The earlier that short-day onions are planted, the larger they get. In the South,

onions can be planted in the fall and overwintered. Since they continue to grow throughout the winter, they will be ready for harvest in the spring.

■ **Intermediate, or day-neutral, onions** are best suited to the middle tier of U.S. states, approximately between latitudes 32° and 42°, and start bulbs when day length reaches 12 to 14 hours.

■ **Long-day onions** grow best in the northern states, between latitudes 37° and 47°, and start bulbs when day length reaches 14 to 16 hours.

Do not . . .

■ *try to fool Mother Nature:* Short-day onions planted in a long-day zone will result in small bulbs—not an early harvest.

■ *confuse day length* (longer in summer in northern areas than in southern areas) *with the length of the growing season* (longer in southern areas than in northern areas).

PLANTING

If you're starting seeds, plant them 8 to 12 weeks before the transplant date (about 2 weeks before the last spring frost; delaying the start can result in miniature onions). Fill potting trays or pots with moist (not soggy) seed-starting mix. Sow seeds on the surface, two to four seeds per square inch. Cover with about ¼ inch of soil and water gently with a spritzer or hand-pump spray bottle. Cover with plastic. Set aside in a place that's 70° to 75°F or place on a heat mat. Following germination, remove the plastic, move the seedlings to a cooler spot, and keep the soil moist.

When the leaves are 5 inches tall, trim them to 2 inches; this will encourage them to grow thicker and stronger. Each day, beginning about 2 weeks before transplanting, expose them to the outdoors for increasingly longer periods. When transplanting, separate them carefully.

Prepare a container that is at least

PLACE THE CONTAINER WHERE IT WILL RECEIVE THE MAXIMUM HOURS OF DIRECT SUNLIGHT.

10 inches deep and as wide as possible (to allow for space between maturing onions). A 5-gallon bucket will support 4 to 6 onions, and a tub many more.

Place the container where it will receive the maximum hours of direct sunlight per day. (It will be heavy to move once filled and planted.)

Provide a well-draining potting mix that is rich in organic matter; add compost or well-rotted manure. Mix in a complete fertilizer, per the package guidance on container size, or fertilize with diluted fish emulsion or compost tea.

Plant sets and transplants 1 to 2 inches deep and 3 to 4 inches apart.

Water gently.

CARE

Water 1 to 2 inches per week.

Mulch the pot to retain moisture.

After about a month, feed the onions a spoonful of ammonium sulfate (21-0-0), or other high-nitrogen fertilizer every 2 to 3 weeks to help plants to produce more foliage and larger bulbs. Stop fertilizing at around the time of the summer solstice (the third week of June), which is the peak day length period.

Water regularly until foliage starts to turn brown and wither—a sign that bulbs are starting to mature. At this time, keep the soil as dry as possible.

DISEASES/PESTS (see pages 184–200)

Although container onions—often being in a compact space and rather isolated from other plantings—are usually less susceptible to diseases and pests than those planted in-ground, here we include some that affect almost all onions, regardless of how planted.

Diseases: Botrytis blight, damping off, downy mildew, pink root, purple blotch, viruses (including iris yellow spot virus), white rot. *Pests:* onion maggots, thrips (onion thrips).

HARVEST/STORAGE

Pull up the onions when the tops are dried, brown, and falling over.

Cure onions by spreading them out in the sun to allow the foliage to dry and the skin to toughen. If the weather is rainy, dry them in a shed, garage, barn, or other protected space. Depending on conditions, curing can take 2 to 4 weeks.

After curing, hang them in a mesh bag or as a braid or spread them in a box no more than two deep in a cool (32° to 40°F), dry, well-ventilated area. Check periodically for sprouting or rotting onions and remove them. Do not store onions in the refrigerator, where conditions are too damp.

Note that sweet onions do not keep well because they have a high water content. To avoid bruising, store them so that they do not touch each other— for example, in clean old panty hose. Slip in the onions one at a time, tying a knot between each one. Hang them in a cool, dry place.

RECOMMENDED VARIETIES

Short-Day

• *Allium cepa* 'Red Creole': heirloom; 3- to 4-inch, dark red globe shape; pungent; resistant to pink root

• *A. cepa* 'White Bermuda', aka 'Crystal Wax', 'Texas Sweet': heirloom cocktail onion; 3- to 4-inch, satiny white, flat shape; originally cultivated in Bermuda in the late 1800s; sweet

• *A. cepa* 'Yellow Granex': Vidalia type; 3- to 4-inch, yellow, flattened globe shape; crisp; said to be the sweetest of the super sweet; resistant to pink root

Intermediate, or Day-Neutral

• *A. cepa* 'Purplette': mini onion, at 1½ inches; glossy, burgundy red when raw; pastel pink when cooked or pickled; mild, sweet

• *A. cepa* 'Southport Yellow Globe': early; 2½- to 3½-inch thick-skin yellow globe; mild, sweet

Long-Day

• *A. cepa* 'Ailsa Craig': heirloom; named for a Scottish island; large, up to 8 inches in diameter; average 2 pounds; pale yellow skin, globe shape; mild, sweet

• *A. cepa* 'Gold Coin': cipollini; 1½- to 3-inch yellow flattened bulb; pungent flavor sweetens when cooked

• *A. cepa* 'Red of Florence': heirloom; 4- to 6-inch long, dark purple-red, torpedo shape; mild, sweet

PEPPERS

Capsicum spp.

**JEALOUSY IS LIKE A HOT PEPPER. USE IT MILDLY,
AND YOU ADD SPICE TO THE RELATIONSHIP.
USE TOO MUCH OF IT, AND IT CAN BURN.**

–Ayala Malach Pines, Israeli psychologist (1945–2012)

Spice up your life! Nearly 2,000 varieties of peppers are cultivated, varying from mild to hot to sweet as candy and ranging in fruit size from 12 inches long (the medium-heat, sweet-tasting 'NuMex Big Jim') to one-third of an inch in diameter (the very hot, berry-like chiltepin).

In most cases, container growers will prefer compact varieties (up to 2 feet tall) over tall ones, which require support and very large containers. Be prepared to search for compact varieties as seedlings; they can be hard to come by. Finding seeds to buy and starting them at home may be easier and more efficient.

Peppers are in the nightshade (Solanaceae) family—making them cousins to tomatoes, eggplants, and potatoes—so they enjoy some of the same conditions.

PLANTING

If you're starting seeds indoors, sow them 8 to 10 weeks before the last spring frost date. Harden off plants when temperatures reach 65°F and set them into containers 2 to 3 weeks after any threat of frost has passed. If you're buying seedlings, choose those with straight, sturdy stems, four to six leaves, and no blooms or fruit.

Prepare containers: Plan to use one plant in each container whose diameter across the top measures at least 12 inches; a pot with an 18-inch diameter may be suitable for two plants. (Crowded plants are poor producers.)

Prepare potting mix by adding compost or organic matter and a slow-release fertilizer (if it is not included in the mix). Water to dampen before planting.

RECOMMENDED VARIETIES

• *Capsicum annuum* 'Bird's Eye', aka Thai: 12- to 18-inch-tall plant bears 1- to 2-inch-long fruit; primarily ornamental but can be eaten (warning: 50,000 to 100,000 Scoville Heat Units, which is hotter than jalapeño, serrano, and cayenne); thrives in heat, humidity

• *C. annuum* 'Early Jalapeño': heirloom; 18- to 26-inch-tall plants produce 3-inch-long, medium hot (2,500 to 5,000 Scoville units) pods; harvest at 65 days (ideal for short-season zones); use green or ripen to sweeter red (chipotle peppers are smoke-dried red jalapeños)

• *C. annuum* 'Fushimi': Japanese heirloom; 24-inch-tall plants produce narrow, 6-inch-long sweet pods; use as original green or ripen to red; crispier than 'Shishito'

• *C. annuum* 'Mini Bell Mix': 15- to 24-inch-tall plants produce 1½x2-inch, thick-wall, sweet bell peppers that ripen to red, orange, or yellow; disease-resistant

• *C. annuum* 'Mini Chocolate Bell': 18- to 24-inch-tall bushy plants produce approximately 2x2-inch, three-lobe, very sweet fruit that ripen to deep brown

• *C. annuum* 'Poblano': heirloom; 30-inch-tall plants produce 4-inch-long fruit with mild heat (1,000 to 2,000 Scoville units); ripen from dark green to rust red (anchos are the dried form)

• *C. annuum* var. *grossum* 'Shishito': Japanese heirloom; 24-inch-tall plants produce 3- to 4-inch-long, slightly wrinkled, sweet-mild peppers (50 to 200 Scoville units); emerald green pods ripen to red

• *C. annuum* 'Sweet Banana': 16- to 24-inch-tall plants produce 6-inch-long fruit that turn yellow to orange to red (ripe) as sweetness increases; disease-resistant

• *C. annuum* 'Sweet Heat': compact, 10- to 12-inch-tall plants bear 3- to 4-inch-long fruit that start green and turn red; mild heat

• *C. annuum* 'Tangerine Dream': 18-inch-tall, bushy plants produce 3-inch-long, sweet orange fruit; mild heat

WIT & WISDOM

● *Developed in 1912 by Wilbur Scoville (1865–1942) and ranging from zero to 16 million Scoville Heat Units, the Scoville scale measures the level of a chile pepper's heat, which is caused by an oil-like compound called capsaicin.*

● *Use caution when handling chile peppers and wear gloves if possible. In any case, try not to touch your eyes or face for several hours afterward.*

CARE

Water 1 to 2 inches per week. Soak the soil thoroughly and allow to almost dry out between waterings. Frequent light watering encourages a weak root system. Water more frequently during hotter weather.

About 2 weeks after planting, begin feeding weekly with a balanced soluble fertilizer.

When the plants begin flowering, introduce a high-potassium, low-nitrogen fertilizer (e.g., 9-15-30) and/or a combination of fish emulsion, kelp meal, and bonemeal.

WHEN WATERING, SOAK THE SOIL, THEN ALLOW TO ALMOST DRY OUT BETWEEN WATERINGS.

DISEASES/PESTS *(see pages 184–200)*

Although container pepper plants—often being in a compact space and rather isolated from other plantings—are usually less susceptible to diseases and pests than those planted in-ground, here we include many that affect almost all peppers, regardless of how planted.

Diseases: anthracnose, blossom-end rot, Phytophthora crown and root rot, powdery mildew, southern bacterial wilt, southern blight, Verticillium wilt, viruses (including cucumber mosaic virus). *Pests:* aphids, Colorado potato beetles, corn earworms (aka tomato fruitworms), flea beetles, root-knot nematodes, thrips, tomato hornworms.

HARVEST/STORAGE

Harvest when peppers ripen completely. Use clippers to remove the fruit, leaving a ¼- to ½-inch stem.

Refrigerate peppers in plastic bags for 1 to 2 weeks.

Peppers can also be dried: Preheat the oven to 140°F. Wash, core, and seed peppers. Cut them into ½-inch strips. Steam for 10 minutes, then spread in a single layer on a baking sheet (lined with parchment paper, if desired) and roast for 4 to 6 hours. Check and turn over peppers occasionally. Cool, then store in bags or containers in the refrigerator.

POTATOES

Solanum tuberosum

PAPA, POTATOES, POULTRY, PRUNES, AND PRISM ARE ALL VERY GOOD WORDS FOR THE LIPS.

–Charles Dickens, English writer (1812–70), in Little Dorrit

The taste and the texture of home-grown potatoes are far superior to those of store-bought spuds—and garden "taters" provide a bounty of nutrients! Potatoes are a cholesterol-free, fat-free source of carbohydrates. Do not discard the skin, which can provide 45% of your vitamin C and 18% of your potassium daily minimum requirements, as well as folate, iron, magnesium, niacin, phosphorus, riboflavin, thiamin, and zinc.

The potato belongs to the nightshade (Solanaceae) family, which includes tomatoes, peppers, and eggplants. The edible part of the potato is the underground "tuber," which serves as an enlarged underground storage area for the potato plant. The tuber develops from underground stems called "stolons" once the plants are 6 to 8 inches tall, or around 5 to 7 weeks after planting.

Potatoes like sunny, cool weather. In warmer climates, they can be grown as a winter crop, with planting times ranging from September to February. Elsewhere, potatoes can be planted 2 weeks before the last spring frost (just be aware that early crops may be ruined by a frost or wet soil)—or later, through April or even in June, depending on location.

PLANTING

Potatoes can occupy a lot of space in small gardens, so large containers are great alternatives. How large? A 32-gallon trash can, being deep and wide, works well, but a container that's 2 to 3 feet tall, with a 10- to 15-gallon capacity, should also be fine.

Set your large container in a place that gets at least 6 hours of sunlight every day. (Once it's full, it will be difficult to move.)

Put a mixture of half compost and half potting mix into the trash can at about 6 to 8 inches deep. Set aside a portion of potting mix for hilling later.

Use certified (disease-resistant) seed potatoes from which eyes (buds) protrude. (Do not confuse seed potatoes with potato seeds or grocery produce.) One to 2 days before planting, cut large seed potatoes into golf ball–size pieces, with 1 to 2 eyes each (this is called "chitting"). The time allows the pieces to heal, or form a protective layer over the cut surface, which improves both moisture retention and rot resistance. Do not cut up seed potatoes that are smaller than a hen's egg; plant them whole.

Place seed potato pieces about 1 foot apart under 3 to 4 inches of soil, with their cut side down. (A 32-gallon trash can should be able to comfortably accommodate four seed potatoes.)

CARE

Water to keep the soil moist but not soggy. Give the plants 1 to 2 inches of water a week. Too much water right after planting and not enough as the potatoes begin to form can cause them to become misshapen.

Sprouts should appear in 14 to 21 days.

A potato crop benefits from added nutrients. Fertilize with a synthetic, high-phosphorus product (e.g., with a middle number such as the 10 in 5-10-10), as phosphorus improves tuber production, or with an organic mix of fish emulsion, kelp meal, and bonemeal per package directions.

As the plants grow, keep their stems covered by adding extra potting mix, mounding or hilling it over the stems so that they are not exposed to sunlight. (Allow the leaves to be exposed.) Hilling keeps potatoes from getting sunburned, which can cause them to turn green. As

RECOMMENDED VARIETIES

Longer-producing than early-season types, mid- and late-season potatoes are usually better container choices.

Early-Season
• *Solanum tuberosum* 'Irish Cobbler': tan skin; irregular shape

Midseason
• *S. tuberosum* 'Red Pontiac': red skin; deep eyes

• *S. tuberosum* 'Purple Viking': mottled purple and red skin; very productive

• *S. tuberosum* 'Red Chieftain': red skin; resistant to common potato scab; stores well

Late-Season
• *S. tuberosum* 'Katahdin': tan skin; resistant to some viruses

• *S. tuberosum* 'Kennebec': tan skin; resistant to some viruses and late blight

• *S. tuberosum* 'Elba': tan skin; large, round tubers; resistant to blights and common potato scab

this happens, they produce a chemical called solanine, which gives off a bitter taste and is toxic.

Stop hilling when about 6 inches of soil has been added around the growing stem and before it blooms.

Stop watering when the foliage withers, wilts, and begins to turn yellow and die off. These are signs that it's nearly time to harvest your potatoes.

DISEASES/PESTS *(see pages 184–200)*
Although container potato plants—often being in a compact space and rather

isolated from other plantings—are usually less susceptible to diseases and pests than those planted in-ground, here we include many that affect almost all potato plants, regardless of how planted.

Diseases: aster yellows ("purple top"), common potato scab, early blight, Fusarium wilt, late blight, southern bacterial wilt, Verticillium wilt, viruses. *Pests:* aphids, Colorado potato beetles, cutworms, flea beetles, leafhoppers, slugs/snails, tomato hornworms, whiteflies, wireworms.

HARVEST/STORAGE
Harvest "new" potatoes—small ones with tender skin—on a dry day 2 to 3 weeks after plants stop flowering. If the soil is very wet, let potatoes air-dry before putting them into bags or baskets. Eat new potatoes within a few days (curing is not necessary); they will not keep for much longer. Harvest larger, more mature potatoes 2 to 3 weeks after the foliage has died.

Place freshly dug potatoes in a cool (45° to 60°F), dry space for up to 2 weeks to allow the skin to cure and the potatoes to thus keep longer. Brush off any clinging soil, then store in a cool (38° to 40°F), somewhat humid, dark place. Do not store potatoes with apples, whose ethylene gas causes potatoes to spoil. Never store potatoes in the refrigerator.

Avoid washing potatoes, which will shorten their storage life.

WIT & WISDOM
- *In New England, growers plant potato crops when dandelions bloom.*
- *Tradition holds that potatoes should be planted on or near March 17, St. Patrick's Day.*
- *Grated raw potato is said to soothe sunburned skin.*

SALAD GREENS

Brassica rapa, Diplotaxis tenuifolia, Eruca sativa, Lactuca sativa, Spinacia oleracea

A SALAD IS NOT A MEAL, IT IS A STYLE.

–Fran Lebowitz, American writer (b. 1950)

What's your salad style? When you grow salad greens in containers, it can be different every day, as there are dozens of lettuce varieties along with other leafy edibles. What's more, greens can grow in as little as 6 inches of soil! Some greens can be harvested in as little as a month's time, and cut-and-come-again plants keep producing, often for weeks! In fact, the hardest part of "salad bowl gardening" may be deciding what to grow.

PLANTING

Consider these options as you plan your salad greens garden and keep an eye out for others:

■ **Asian greens** include mizuna, which produces bunches of thin, frilly leaves, and tatsoi, which has mild-tasting green leaves that form a small mound.

■ **Baby kale,** which produces mild, tender leaves, is bred to grow about 4 inches tall. Seeds may be packaged as one variety or a mix of several.

■ **Butterhead lettuces,** which form loose heads with soft leaves, include the Bibb and Boston types.

■ **Cos, aka romaine, lettuces** form loose heads of long, semi-folded leaves with thick midribs.

■ **Crisp head lettuces** include 'Iceberg', which forms a firm, or crisp, head of leaves.

■ **Loose-leaf lettuces** have a center stalk, with leaves loosely arranged on it. These grow quickly, maturing in as few as 45 days (baby leaves can be picked sooner). The leaves tend to be soft and

crinkled types. Smooth-leaf varieties are usually eaten fresh, while crinkled-leaf spinach is preferable for cooking. Spinach has greater tolerance for cool temperatures than most lettuces, but it has little tolerance for heat and long days, being inclined to bolt.

Some greens thrive in the cool seasons, while others prefer summerlike temperatures. Consult your seed packet for details about each plant's best season as well as other specific planting guidance.

Choose a container that is 6 to 12 inches deep; a diameter of 18 inches is

SOME GREENS THRIVE IN THE COOL SEASONS, WHILE OTHERS PREFER SUMMERLIKE TEMPERATURES.

range in color from greens to reds to combinations thereof.

■ **Mesclun** is a blend of lettuces and greens. You can buy packaged seeds or make your own mesclun mix.

■ **Mustard greens, including arugula (aka rocket),** have a tangy, peppery flavor. These also bolt (go to seed) quickly in warm weather. Arugula is available as mildly peppery, "standard" or salad varieties or as spicier "wild" types.

■ **Spinach leaves** include smooth and

recommended. (Greater depth allows more room for roots and keeps the soil from drying out.)

Moisten (do not soak) a portion of good-quality potting mix—enough to fill your container to within an inch of the top.

Direct-sow seeds densely—about ½ inch apart—on the prepared mix. Then cover with about ¼ inch of dry potting mix, sprinkling it around. Tamp, or press, the seeds gently (a flat surface is recommended) so that they make contact

RECOMMENDED VARIETIES

Asian Greens

- *Brassica rapa* var. *nipposinica:* mizuna; a traditional Japanese vegetable; numerous varieties and shades of green, pink, purple, and red; deeply serrated/frilly leaves (up to 200 stems); baby leaves appear in about 3 weeks; choose from seasonal varieties

- *B. rapa* var. *rosularis:* tatsoi; spoon-shape leaves form low-growing rosettes 12 inches in diameter; cool-season crop; drought-tolerant; high in Vitamin C

Baby Kale

- *Brassica* Kalebration kale mix: a blend of types and colors (depending on availability)

- *B. oleracea* var. *palmifolia* 'Tuscan Baby Leaf': heirloom; fast-growing (25 days); "cut-and-come-again" style

Baby Spinach

- *Spinacia oleracea* 'Baby Leaf Riverside': hybrid; spade-shape leaves; cool-season crop; resistant to downy mildew

- *S. oleracea* 'Space': hybrid; fast-growing (25 days); heat-tolerant; slow to bolt; resistant to downy mildew; a true three-season spinach

Butterhead

- *Lactuca sativa* 'Merveille des Quatre Saisons': French for "marvel of the four seasons"; heirloom; crisp green outer leaves tipped with deep red; rosette head; frost-hardy; slow to bolt; can be grown almost year-round

- *L. sativa* 'Tom Thumb': heirloom; 3- to 4-inch-diameter heads (the size of a tennis ball); bright-green outer leaves, creamy yellow interior; frost-hardy

Loose-Leaf

- *L. sativa* 'Red Salad Bowl': heirloom; large, oakleaf variety; wide, maroon-red, deeply lobed leaves; slow to bolt

- *L. sativa* 'Royal Oakleaf': heirloom; 10- to 14-inch-long green leaves resemble oak leaves; performs well in heat and cold; resists turning bitter

Mesclun

- *L. sativa:* mesclun; from the French *mesclar,* for "merge" or "mix"; seed packets contain a blend of lettuce and greens (depending on availability); often can be harvested in as few as 30 days

Mustard Greens

- *Eruca sativa:* arugula, aka rocket or roquette; standard variety; fast-growing (21 days); 3- to 6-inch height; deeply lobed dark leaves; cool-season crop

- *Diplotaxis tenuifolia* 'Dragon's Fire': wild mustard variety; zesty flavor; red veins on green lobed leaves; vigorous, uniform growth habit; harvest at 2 to 6 inches tall

Romaine

- *L. sativa* 'Forellenschluss': from the Austrian German for "speckled like a trout"; heirloom; medium green leaves with wine-red or maroon splotches; cool-season crop

- *L. sativa* 'Little Gem', aka 'Sucrine' or 'Sugar Cos': heirloom; sweetness of a butterhead; 5 to 6 inches tall; dense, tight head

WIT & WISDOM

• *'Iceberg' lettuce got its name when, in the early 1900s, California growers realized that it would "keep" while being transported across the country if it were covered in crushed ice. Until then, it had been called 'Crisphead'.*

• *If you find the taste of raw kale to be too bitter, try giving it a massage. Remove stems and then chop leaves into pieces. Add a small amount of lemon juice or olive oil, then use your fingers to rub the leaves together for several minutes until the kale begins to wilt.*

with the soil and to keep them from blowing away. Water gently (a handheld pump container is advised instead of a hose, the water force from which can displace the cover soil and seeds).

Keep the seedbed moist. (You can assess the wetness of the container by lifting it, as it will be lighter when dry.)

CARE

Provide 4 to 6 hours of sunlight per day.

When seedlings are 4 to 6 inches tall, apply a balanced fertilizer at half strength. Continue watering as needed. Apply diluted fertilizer every 2 weeks, or per package directions.

Protect greens from afternoon sun, if necessary and especially in summer, with shade cloth or row cover or by moving containers into shade.

Plant more seeds in other containers every 2 to 4 weeks to maintain a fresh crop.

DISEASES/PESTS *(see pages 184–200)*

Although container greens—often being in a compact space and rather isolated from other plantings—are usually less susceptible to diseases and pests than those planted in-ground, here we include many that can affect a number of salad greens (but most notably kale, lettuce, and spinach), regardless of how planted.

Diseases: black root rot, damping

off, downy mildew, fungal leaf spot (including Alternaria and Cercospora leaf spots), powdery mildew, Sclerotinia white mold, viruses [including cucumber mosaic virus (aka spinach blight) and lettuce mosaic virus], white rust. *Pests:* aphids, cabbage loopers, cutworms, flea beetles, imported cabbageworms, leaf miners, slugs/snails, whiteflies.

HARVEST/STORAGE

Harvest times vary, depending on the type of plant—for instance, loose-leaf (at 4 to 6 inches) vs. romaine and head lettuces (65 to 75 days after planting). Leaves of arugula, kale, mesclun, mizuna, and spinach—plus, if desired, exterior butterhead leaves—can be harvested when plants are 4 to 6 inches tall. Use scissors to make a clean cut and avoid loosening the plant in the soil. In order to "cut-and-come-again," retain several leaves within an inch of the plant base to encourage regrowth. To harvest head lettuces, slice them off at the root base.

Store lettuce in a plastic bag in the refrigerator for up to 10 days. When ready to use, soak in cold water for a few minutes, then drain on a towel or spin in a salad spinner.

Lettuce leaves wilted? Put them in a bowl of cold water with ice cubes and soak for about 15 minutes. Spin as above.

SQUASHES

Cucurbita spp.

**TOMATOES AND SQUASHES NEVER FAIL TO REACH
MATURITY. YOU CAN SPRAY THEM WITH ACID, BEAT THEM
WITH STICKS, AND BURN THEM; THEY LOVE IT.**

–S. J. Perelman, American humorist (1904–79)

Squashes are popular and prolific vegetables to grow. The ever-increasing number of compact varieties suited for containers provide options for any taste and space.

Squashes are one of two types: bush or vining. Bush types tend to be smaller (take up less space), faster-growing plants; most mature in 75 to 85 days. Sprawling vining plants tend to mature in 100 days or more. Bush plants are generally better suited to containers, but in a large pot with space to spread, vining squashes can produce a successful harvest.

Squashes are generally divided into two categories: summer and winter.

■ **Summer squashes** include pattypan, yellow, and zucchini; each type yields throughout its season. The skin on these veggies tends to be tender and flavorful.

■ **Winter squashes**—acorn, butternut,

pumpkin, and spaghetti—produce fruit that are usually harvested at around the same time. These produce sweet creamy flesh under tough, thick rinds that protect them from frost and enable long storage.

PLANTING

Prepare a 5-gallon or 14-inch-diameter pot with rich potting mix for each variety of squash that you want to grow.

When the soil temperature reaches around 70°F, or 2 weeks after the last frost date, direct-sow two seeds of the same variety 1 inch deep into the container and water to dampen. (Transplant homegrown or purchased seedlings if you want to jump-start the growing season.) Following germination, remove the weaker plant by cutting its stem; this is less disturbing to the roots.

Water regularly to keep soil moist. If you're growing vining squashes, insert a trellis into the container for the plant to climb later.

CARE

Provide 6 to 8 hours of sun per day.

About 6 weeks after the seeds have been planted, apply fertilizer. After the first true leaves appear (those after the initial two), apply a slow-release pellet fertilizer, according to the label's directions. Follow up with a weekly dose of balanced fertilizer, based on the label's guidance for the pot size.

When watering, avoid getting water on the leaves. Water the soil 1 inch per week directly or set the container in a bucket or tub of water and allow it to be absorbed.

As the plants grow, train the vines (if that type) onto the trellis or other support. Use string to gently secure them.

RECOMMENDED VARIETIES

Summer
• *Cucurbita pepo* 'Astia': zucchini; compact vines produce 6- to 7-inch-long fruit among ornamental silvery-green leaves; resistant to powdery mildew

• *C. pepo* var. *clypeata* 'Sunburst': pattypan; vining 3-foot bush produces several dozen brilliant yellow fruit per plant; best when harvested at 2 to 3 inches long

Winter
• *C. moschata* 'Butterscotch': butternut; vining plant produces four or more 6-inch-long (1- to 2-pound) fruit per plant; resistant to powdery mildew

• *C. moschata* 'Honeybaby': butternut; vining plant produces around nine lightbulb-shape, 6- to 7-inch-long (4- to 8-ounce) fruit per plant; resistant to powdery mildew

• *C. pepo* 'Honey Bear': acorn; 2- to 3-foot-tall plant produces three to five 1-pound fruit per bush

WIT & WISDOM

- *The word "squash" comes from the Narragansett indigenous people's word* askutasquash, *which means "eaten raw or uncooked."*
- *Squash is technically a fruit because it contains the plant's seeds, but for culinary purposes, it is treated as a vegetable.*

DISEASES/PESTS *(see pages 184–200)*

Although container squash plants—often being in a compact space and rather isolated from other plantings—are usually less susceptible to diseases and pests than those planted in-ground, here we include many that can affect a number of squashes, regardless of how planted.

Diseases: angular leaf spot, bacterial wilt, blossom-end rot, downy mildew, Phytophthora crown and root rot, powdery mildew, Sclerotinia white mold, viruses (including cucumber mosaic virus). *Pests:* aphids, cucumber beetles, squash bugs, squash vine borers, stinkbugs, thrips.

HARVEST/STORAGE

For the best quality, pick summer squashes at maturity, when their skin is glossy and body firm but not hard. Use pruners or a sharp knife to avoid damaging the vines. Handle with care, as the fruit bruise easily. Store in the crisper drawer of the refrigerator and use within a few days.

Harvest winter squashes in autumn, before the first heavy frost. Use pruners or a sharp knife to cut the stem, leaving about 2 inches, if possible, on most and 3 to 4 inches on pumpkins. Handle with care: In order for winter squashes to store well, their rinds must be firm, without bruising or skin breaks. Cure winter

FOR THE BEST QUALITY, PICK SUMMER SQUASHES AT MATURITY, WHEN THEY ARE TENDER AND AT THEIR PREDICTED SIZE.

squashes (except acorn) in a warm (80° to 85°F), humid (80% to 85%) room for 10 to 14 days. Store them in a cool (50° to 55°F), dry, well-ventilated location away from ripening fruit.

SWEET POTATOES

Ipomoea batatas

SWEET POTATOES ARE IDEAL FOR LAZY DAYS: JUST BAKE, THEN MASH AND MIX WITH YOGURT, BUTTER, OR OLIVE OIL.

–Yotam Ottolenghi, Israeli-born English chef and restaurateur (b. 1968)

Sweet potatoes are not related to regular white potatoes, which are in the nightshade (Solanaceae) family; "sweets" belong instead to the morning glory family, Convolvulaceae. Their heart-shape leaves are a reminder of that relationship. They are not a tuber but a fleshy root, native to Central and South America. Being tropical vegetables, they are usually grown in southern states but can produce a harvest in northern areas, with some planning.

PLANTING

Bush-type sweet potato plants are ideal for container growers. The vines that they produce are short and compact, not sprawling like typical sweets—but the roots are full size, not miniatures.

Sweets grow not from seeds but from

slips (shoots), which can be purchased or started from organically grown sweets purchased at a grocery or farmers' market. (Be sure to ask about the variety and note it.) Six to 8 weeks before your last frost date, poke three or four toothpicks into the middle (waist) of the sweet. Then suspend it on the toothpicks in a glass of water so that the sweet is halfway submerged. When the slips are 6 to 12 inches long, remove them, with roots attached, for planting.

While slips mature, prepare a large container or tub. (A too-small container can result in small, curly sweets or fewer than hoped for.) A 10-gallon container can support two or three sweet potatoes; a 20-gallon one, four to six. A half-barrel container (20 to 25 gallons) is ideal. Place the container where it will receive full sunlight every day. (It will be heavy to move once filled and planted.)

Sweets like moist but not wet soil; the medium must be well-draining and rich; sweets are also heavy feeders. Provide potting mix amended with compost, sand, bonemeal (for potassium), and wood ash (for potash). Minimize nitrogen or risk producing heavily leafy tops and spindly roots.

If you purchase a bush variety, soak the roots in water for a few hours before planting.

RECOMMENDED VARIETIES

Bush

• *Ipomoea batatas* 'Bush Porto Rico': heirloom; 110 days; 6 to 12 inches tall; red roots with yellow-to-orange flesh; generous yields

• *I. batatas* 'Vardaman': 110 days; 6 to 10 inches tall; golden yellow roots with reddish-orange, sweet flesh; purple leaves; not finicky about soil or climate

Running (or Vining)

• *I. batatas* 'Beauregard': heirloom; 90 days; vines to about 40 inches; large, uniform, red-skin roots, deep orange inside; common among commercial growers; crack-resistant

Plant slips 3 to 4 weeks after the last spring frost, when the soil has warmed to 65°F and nighttime temperatures are at least 55°F. Mulch with black plastic before and during the season, if necessary, to capture or retain heat. Set slips 4 inches deep on a bed of compost, then cover up to their bottom leaves.

Water with a high-phosphorus liquid fertilizer (5-10-10) for 7 to 10 days to ensure that the plants root well.

WIT & WISDOM

• *Do not confuse sweet potatoes and yams. True yams are from the Dioscoreaceae plant family. They are huge tubers with a rough, scaly skin that are grown mostly in West Africa and tropical Asia, where they can get the 8- to 10-month-long growing season that they need to mature. Yams can grow to be 3 to 4 feet long and weigh up to 80 pounds!*

CARE

Although sweet potatoes are drought-resistant, for best results, water regularly. Plan to provide about 3 gallons of water per plant per week. Include or add compost tea once per month.

Protect from any late frosts or cooler nights with a blanket or row covers.

Late in the season, reduce watering to avoid cracking the sweet's skin—a problem in storage.

DISEASES/PESTS *(see pages 184–200)*

Although container sweet potato plants—often being in a compact space and rather isolated from other plantings—are usually less susceptible to diseases and pests than those planted in-ground, here we include many that can affect a number of sweet potatoes, regardless of how planted.

Diseases: Fusarium wilt (stem rot), southern bacterial wilt, sweet potato scurf, viruses (including sweet potato feathery mottle virus, aka internal cork), white rust. *Pests:* aphids, flea beetles, root-knot nematodes, sweet potato weevils, whiteflies, wireworms.

HARVEST/STORAGE

The signal to harvest is yellowing leaves. Loosen the soil and cut away some vines. Pull up the plant's primary crown and dig out the sweets by hand. Alternately, tip the container on its side, pour out the contents, and carefully harvest the sweets (they bruise easily). Shake off excess soil; do not wash the sweets.

Sweet potatoes must be cured to bring out their sweetness. Place them in a well-ventilated, warm (80° to 90°F), humid (85% to 90%) place for 10 to 14 days, then store them in a cool (60°F), dry place. Do not refrigerate or store below 50°F.

WHILE SLIPS MATURE, PREPARE A LARGE CONTAINER OR TUB.

TOMATOES

Solanum lycopersicum

**A WORLD WITHOUT TOMATOES IS
LIKE A STRING QUARTET WITHOUT VIOLINS.**

–Laurie Colwin, American writer (1944–92)

Cue the music for America's favorite vegetable! Tomatoes are relatively easy to grow, and many varieties are especially suited for containers. In northern regions, tomato plants need at least 6 hours of sunlight daily; 8 to 10 hours are preferred. In southern regions, light afternoon shade (natural or applied, e.g., row covers) will help tomatoes to survive and thrive.

PLANTING
DETERMINE THE TYPE:
■ **Determinate,** better known as "bush," varieties grow 3 to 4 feet tall. These plants are ideal for containers and small spaces. This type tends to provide numerous ripe tomatoes at one time, does not put on much vegetative/leaf growth after setting fruit, and tends to fruit for a (relatively) brief period of

time. They are generally less productive in the latter part of the growing season. Determinate tomatoes do not require staking or caging.

■ **Indeterminate,** better known as "vining," varieties produce the largest types of mid- to late-season slicing tomatoes all summer long and until the first frost. Indeterminate tomatoes need 5-gallon or larger pots and staking.

GROWING TOMATOES IN POTS

Use a large pot or container (at least 20 inches in diameter) and loose,

HARVEST RED TOMATOES WHEN
THEY ARE FIRM AND VERY
RED, REGARDLESS OF SIZE.

well-draining soil (e.g., at least 12 inches of a good potting mix with added organic matter). To the potting mix, apply a slow-release pelleted fertilizer per the rate on the package label.

Choose bush (determinate) or dwarf varieties. Many cherry tomatoes grow well in pots. Taller varieties may need staking. Plant one tomato plant per pot.

CARE

Provide 8 hours of sunlight per day, if possible.

Water in the early morning so that plants have sufficient moisture to make it through a hot day. Water generously in the first few days and then with about 2 inches per week during the growing season. Keep the soil moist. Check daily and provide extra water during heat waves. Deep watering encourages a strong root system. Avoid overhead and afternoon watering.

Tomatoes benefit from added nutrients. About 2 weeks after planting, water weekly with a balanced soluble fertilizer such as 20-20-20. When plants begin flowering, switch to a high-potassium formula such as 9-15-30. Supplement with liquid seaweed or fish emulsion every 2 weeks, starting when vining tomatoes are about 1 inch in diameter. Avoid high-nitrogen fertilizer unless plants have yellow leaves. Too much nitrogen will result in lush foliage but few flowers and little or no fruit. If plants have purple leaves, fertilize with phosphorus.

If you are growing vining tomatoes, pinch off suckers (new, tiny stems and leaves between branches and the main

RECOMMENDED VARIETIES

Tomatoes grow in all sizes, from tiny "currant" to "cherry" to large "beefsteak." There are thousands of tomato varieties to suit different climates and tastes—and new ones are introduced every year. These are especially well-suited to container growing.

Beefsteak
• *Solanum lycopersicum* 'Galahad': 4-foot-tall plant produces meaty, round, red 3-inch fruit weighing about 12 ounces each; determinate

Cherry
Most indeterminate cherry tomatoes can be grown in containers. Use one plant per 5-gallon (or larger) bucket and be prepared to provide support. Several varieties of determinate cherry tomato plants have been bred specifically for container growing. These are prolific producers:

• *S. lycopersicum* 'Baby Boomer': 20 to 25 inches tall; red, cherry-size fruit; resistant to Fusarium wilt, Verticillium wilt; plan to cage the plant; determinate

• *S. lycopersicum* 'Lizzano': 16 to 20 inches tall; red, cherry-size fruit; resistant to late blight; also suitable for hanging baskets; semi-determinate

• *S. lycopersicum* 'Patio Choice': 15 to 18 inches tall; yellow, cherry-size fruit; resistant to Fusarium wilt; determinate

• *S. lycopersicum* var. *cerasiforme* 'Sweet 'n' Neat': 10 to 12 inches tall; red, cherry-size fruit in clumps like grapes; determinate habit, indeterminate producer

• *S. lycopersicum* var. *cerasiforme* 'Terenzo': 16 to 20 inches tall; red, cherry-size fruit; semi-cascading form also suitable for hanging baskets; determinate

• *S. lycopersicum* 'Totem': 18 to 30 inches tall; red, small to medium-size fruit; determinate

• *S. lycopersicum* 'Tumbling Tom': 20 to 24 inches tall; red or yellow cherry-size fruit; resistant to Fusarium wilt, root-knot nematodes, Verticillium wilt; cascading form suitable for hanging baskets; determinate

Roma
• *S. lycopersicum* 'Early Resilience': 24 inches tall; 2-inch-long, 3.5-ounce fruit; highly resistant to blossom-end rot; determinate

stem). This aids air circulation and allows more sunlight into the middle of the plant. Provide support. If necessary, gently tie the stems to stakes with rags, nylon stockings, twine, or soft string. As a plant grows, trim the lower leaves from the bottom 12 inches of the stem.

If no flowers form, plants may not be getting enough sun or water (too little can stop flowering). Flower drop-off could be due to high daytime temperatures (over 90°F). Provide shade

WIT & WISDOM

- *The various varieties of tomato range in size from as large as grapefruits to as small as marbles.*
- *Compact tomato plants may be referred to as "dwarf," "micro," or "patio."*

during the hottest part of the day by using row covers or shade cloth.

If plants produce a lot of flowers but no fruit, the causes might be inadequate light, too little water or inconsistent watering, too cold or hot temperatures, and/or not enough pollinators. Low humidity can also affect pollination; the ideal is 40% to 70%. If humidity is low, mist the plant to help pollen to stick.

DISEASES/PESTS *(see pages 184–200)*
Although container tomato plants—often

IF HUMIDITY IS LOW, MIST THE PLANT
TO HELP POLLEN TO STICK.

being in a compact space and rather isolated from other plantings—are usually less susceptible to diseases and pests than those planted in-ground, here we include many that can affect a number of tomatoes, regardless of how planted.

Diseases: anthracnose, blossom-end rot, cracking, damping off, early blight, Fusarium wilt, late blight, powdery mildew, southern bacterial wilt, Verticillium wilt, viruses (including cucumber mosaic virus, tobacco mosaic virus, tomato mosaic virus). *Pests:* aphids, Colorado potato beetles, corn earworms (aka tomato fruitworms), cutworms, flea beetles, leaf miners, root-knot nematodes, slugs/snails, stinkbugs, tomato hornworms, whiteflies.

HARVEST/STORAGE
Leave tomatoes on the vine for as long as possible. Harvest red tomatoes when they are firm and very red, regardless of size, with perhaps some yellow remaining around the stem. Harvest tomatoes of other colors—orange, purple, yellow, or another rainbow shade—when they turn the correct color.

Never place tomatoes on a sunny windowsill to ripen; they may rot before they are ripe!

Never refrigerate fresh tomatoes. Doing so spoils the flavor and texture that gives them that garden tomato taste.

HOW DOES MY EDIBLE GARDEN GROW?

VARIETY	SOURCE	YEAR PLANTED

You can use *The Old Farmer's Almanac* Garden Planner software to perform dozens of different planning tasks, including figuring out which complementary companion plants or pots should go together. Get a free 7-day trial at GardenPlanner.Almanac.com.

GROW HERBS IN CONTAINERS

FRESH HERBS REALLY BELONG ANYWHERE THAT YOU PUT THEM.

–Alex Guarnaschelli, American chef (b. 1969)

If you're growing vegetables, plan to cultivate a few culinary herbs for use in the kitchen with your veggies. Most grow as well in containers as they do in-ground, provided that they have the proper conditions.

BASIL: This culinary favorite is an annual that requires rich potting mix (aka "soil") and a sunny, warm location. Pinch out spikes of flowers to encourage leaf growth and bushiness and prevent the plant from going to seed. Sow seeds in pots outdoors in a sheltered sunny location or purchase seedlings and transplant with care; basil doesn't like to have its roots disturbed. Plants may grow up to 3 feet tall; purple varieties have a clove-like taste. Harvest throughout the season as needed.

CHIVES: A member of the onion family, this hardy perennial thrives in rich, moist soil in a sunny site but will tolerate some shade. Grow from seeds, bulbs, or division. Chives grow to a height of 4 to 24 inches. Leaves and flowers are edible. Harvest leaves by cutting, not pulling, from the outer edges of the plant. Divide plants every few years to encourage fuller plants.

CILANTRO: This cool-season annual can range from 6 to 30 inches tall when mature. Sow seeds per package directions

HERB BASICS

• Most herbs prefer full sun (at least 6 hours of direct sunlight), but some can tolerate partial shade (2 to 4 hours of sunlight).

• Almost any type of container will do, but herbs will be most successful when the pots are at least 8 inches in diameter, with adequate drainage holes.

• Avoid the urge to pack a pot with plants; if they're crowded, the plants are less likely to thrive and reach their full potential.

• If you're planting more than one herb in one pot, make sure that the plants are compatible. For example, parsley and chives prefer relatively moist soil, while rosemary and thyme like to dry out between soaks.

• Herbs benefit from slow-release fertilizers, especially liquid seaweed products.

• Herbs should be harvested regularly during the growing season to promote continuous growth. With the exception of herbs that grow straight from the ground, such as chives, avoid picking stems from a plant's base; instead, focus on the top of the stem above a pair of leaves and pinch off an inch or two (depending on the plant's size). This will promote bushy growth and discourage lanky stems. Also pinch off any flowers that appear on herbs, as this signals them to continue producing.

in spring or fall in full sun to partial shade. Avoid excess fertilizer. Cutting leaves (harvesting) frequently will extend the harvest but only so much: This short-lived favorite will bolt (flower) quickly in hot weather. The golden-brown seeds are called coriander. Slow-bolting varieties are available.

DILL: This biennial herb grows deep and tall: Grow it in a pot that is at least 12 inches deep to allow for its taproot; its hollow stems will stand 2 to 3 feet tall (provide support, if necessary). Sow seeds in containers in full sun after all danger of frost has passed. Harvest the feathery leaves at any time and keep cutting to promote new growth. If stressed (by

excessive drought or heat), dill may skip its leaf stage and become leggy. Dill self-seeds; avoid "dillweed" in the following season by removing seed heads before they disperse (cut them into a paper bag).

MINT: Many varieties of this aromatic perennial herb are available, and all share similar traits: They have square stems; thrive almost anywhere but prefer moist soil and partial sun; and are invasive when planted in-ground—which is the best reason to grow them in a container. They can grow to be 1 to 4 feet tall. Propagate from cuttings or grow from transplant. (Seeds are not true to type.)

OREGANO: This hardy perennial does well in

containers, growing up to 2 feet tall in full sun. Grow it from seeds or cuttings. Regular watering is critical while seeds are starting and when seedlings are young. When about 4 inches tall, pinch or trim stems to encourage bushiness. The flavor is best before the plant flowers; harvest often but not more than one-third of the plant at a time. Many varieties are available, but Greek *Origanum vulgare* var. *hirtum* is the most popular for cooking.

PARSLEY: This biennial can grow 12 to 30 inches tall. Grow from seeds (soak seeds for 1 to 2 hours before planting to aid/encourage germination) or transplants, disturbing the roots as little as

PARSLEY

ROSEMARY

SAGE

FRENCH TARRAGON

possible, in sunlight or light shade in rich, moist potting mix. Harvest as needed, taking stems from the outer edge first. The common varieties are curly leaf, which is often used as garnish, and flat-leaf (aka Italian), which is preferred for culinary use.

ROSEMARY: This drought-tolerant evergreen perennial shrub loves a container that gets full sun and is full of well-draining potting mix (allow to dry out between waterings). Grow from cuttings taken in spring or transplant established plants. To encourage growth (3 to 4 feet tall), prune hard in spring. Harvest throughout the summer and cut back plants after flowering. There are many varieties of the shrub and ground-hugging types. All rosemary varieties are suitable for cooking, but 'Tuscan Blue' is a culinary favorite.

SAGE: This evergreen perennial grows 1 to 3 feet tall and does best in a sunny location. For best results, take cuttings from an established plant about 3 months before the last spring frost and plant in containers in potting mix. Keep plants moist until they become established. Harvest leaves throughout the summer; large ones are the most flavorful. After flowers pass, cut the plant back to encourage leaf growth, leaving it 3 inches tall.

TARRAGON, FRENCH: This perennial herb is best grown from stem cuttings or root division. Divide the roots after the last spring frost by pulling (not cutting) them apart. Plants grow to be 18 to 36 inches tall and do best in warm, well-draining soil. Avoid Russian tarragon, known as "false tarragon"; it is not as flavorful as the French variety.

VOICE OF EXPERIENCE

I planted oregano in the spring of 2019. It was a wonderful healthy plant that gave me an abundance of oregano to dry, bag, and freeze. I shared it with my relatives, which made all of us happy. It overwintered nicely because we had a mild winter. So, this year, at about the end of June, I decided to let half of my plant bolt and go to seed. (1) It is so beautiful, with the abundance of tiny white flowers that keep coming and coming. More important, (2) the bees love it. I can tell you about 40 bees are on that oregano plant from the instant it gets warm enough for them until it's time for them to "hole up" every single day. I never realized what a great pollinator plant oregano was. I will be harvesting seeds and putting them in my wildflower/pollinator garden here in Zone 6 in Idaho.   —*Frances G., via Almanac.com*

MY CONTAINER HERBS

PLANT	PLANTING DATE	OBSERVATIONS

FRUIT AT YOUR FINGERTIPS

THE TREES THAT ARE SLOW TO GROW BEAR THE BEST FRUIT.

–Jean-Baptiste Poquelin, aka Molière, French playwright (1622–73)

People who grow fruit in containers and actually see their plants produce a harvest seem to have a magic touch—especially to those who try to do it and fail. If that's you, take heart: Success is at your fingertips. If you choose the proper variety, provide the correct growing conditions, and give things time, you will enjoy the fruit of your labor—literally.

BERRIES

BLUE-RIBBON BLUEBERRIES:

As if utter lusciousness weren't enough, blueberries also brim with antioxidants, those magical compounds that help us to live long, healthy lives.

The two main container types are northern highbush (*Vaccinium corymbosum*), hardy in Zones 4 to 8, and the more heat-tolerant rabbiteye (*V. ashei,* aka *V. virgatum*), for Zones 8 to 10.

Most northern highbushes are self-pollinating, while rabbiteyes require cross-pollination from two different varieties. Plants can grow 6 feet tall and wide and, as a

bonus, dazzle with scarlet fall foliage. Then there is 'Blueberry Glaze' blueberry, a *Vaccinium* hybrid that forms a 2-foot compact mound, looks like a boxwood, and can be sheared as such after berries are harvested. Perfect for a container, the shrub has tiny,

deep-green leaves, white-with-pink blossoms in the spring, and small, deep-blue berries in midsummer. Their intense flavor is much like that of wild blueberries. The plant needs 600 chilling hours and grows well in Zones 5 to 8.

Although generally un-demanding and productive, blueberries do require a quite acidic growing medium with a pH between 4.0 and 5.5. Select

semidwarf (3 to 4 feet tall) or dwarf (1 to 2 feet) types bred specifically for containers, such as 'Jelly Bean', 'Pink Icing', 'Pink Sorbet', and 'Top Hat'. Plant these self-pollinators in potting mix and feed lightly with an organic, acid-forming fertilizer. Blueberry pots are quite handsome, so add them to your garden as you would other pots.

STRAWBERRY SHORTCUT: If you want fresh fruit quickly, plant strawberries, as they usually bear in the first year. These vining plants make marvelous hanging baskets that are easy to move and protect from berry thieves. Begin with certified, disease-free plants. You have three types from which to choose: June-bearing (length-of-day sensitive; one main crop in late spring and early summer), everbearing (crops in spring, summer, and fall), and day-neutral (fruiting not determined by day length; produce continuously if temperatures remain between 40° and 85°F; try 'Tristar').

The latter two—everbearing and day-neutral—produce long runners and are ideal for baskets. Enrich the potting mix with ¼ cup of slow-release fertilizer and place three plants in a 10-inch hanging basket. Strawberry plants naturally decline after a couple of years. When they do, replace them and the old potting mix, too.

CITRUS

Citrus has issues: You can't grow it outdoors year-round in most of the country. Plus, homegrown citrus is often limited or banned in states with huge citrus industries like California, Florida, and Arizona, for fear of spreading serious diseases and pests. Still, you do have options.

KUMQUATS: Kumquats are characterized by their slightly sour taste, so you may wish to choose 'Meiwa' because it is sweeter than other varieties and best for eating fresh off the tree. It does well in containers, as do 'Eustis' and 'Nagami'.

While these olive-size fruit can be eaten whole, skin and all, they are frequently used in cooking, such as in making jam or a fruit tart, where their sour taste will temper sweeter fruit.

With proper care, fruit will appear within 2 to 3 years. The fruit begin to ripen in early winter and may continue throughout early spring. Leave fruit on the tree until fully ripe; they will not continue to ripen off the tree. Prune trees after the fruit have set.

LEMONS: Growing lemons in a pot that you bring indoors for winter is pretty cool. For best results (harvest, flavor, raves), choose 'Improved Meyer Lemon', which is an abundant producer with sweeter fruit than many other varieties. The compact plant produces blooms that are pale lavender before they open and turn to white when in full flower. Trees blossom primarily in late winter or early spring and bear fruit in the fall. To maintain shape and size, prune plants in spring after the first round of blossoms appears. Keep the crown from becoming so dense that it blocks sunlight to lower branches and prevents adequate air circulation.

LIMES: Dwarf Bearss seedless and makrut limes are well suited to container growing. Dwarf Bearss has a compact crown and from winter to early spring produces lemon-size fruit best used in drinks and cooking. Makrut limes have a bumpy green skin. Use their leaves, zest, and juice in any recipes that call for limes. Try the Australian finger lime *(Citrus australasica),* which bears finger-shape fruit year-round that contain juice "packets," or vesicles, that burst open inside your mouth. This grows to about 1 foot tall and is an excellent choice for containers. The plant produces black, green, purple, red, or yellow fruit, about 2 inches long, that bloom in autumn. The scent of the fragrant blossoms is a cross between those of gardenia and

jasmine. Limes can be pruned anytime to control growth and shape, but it is best not to cut back the crown all at once. Always leave some growth from the previous year, as buds form on the old growth.

MANDARINS: Mandarins, tangerines, and clementines are all types of mandarin orange. Satsuma mandarins are a good choice for containers. They are also among the most cold-tolerant, disease-resistant, and flavorful varieties. The Satsuma mandarin 'Owari' ripens early and can tolerate temperatures down to 28°F; it reaches to 4 to 6 feet tall in pots. Flavorful 'Dancy' is another cold-hardy and disease-resistant variety. Young plants should be pruned after they flower in the spring to encourage stronger branches. Once established, prune to remove all dead or diseased branches.

GETTING STARTED WITH CITRUS

Choose a tree that stays naturally small or is grafted onto a dwarfing rootstock. Buy trees that are at least 1 year old; 2- to 3-year-old trees are even better. Varieties that have been grafted onto a dwarf rootstock, such as *Citrus trifoliata* 'Flying Dragon', ensure that the trees will be naturally dwarfed and better suited to container growing. Pick plants with plenty of glossy green leaves and avoid those with bare stems or dry, curly, or yellow leaves.

Start by fulfilling the two essentials: at least 6 hours of direct sunlight daily and potting mix amended with perlite, vermiculite, or compost. Next, choose fruit varieties that do well in your climate—plant disease- and pest-resistant varieties if you can. (Your local Cooperative Extension service can advise you on both; to find yours, go to Almanac.com/cooperative-extension-services.) Citrus trees prefer deep, infrequent watering (once or twice a week); avoid overwatering. Water requirements will vary, depending on whether the pot is outdoors or inside, the sunlight, and the temperature. A good rule of thumb is to water only if the soil about 5 to 6 inches below the surface is dry. If the leaves turn yellow, wilt, and begin to drop, this may be due to overwatering, a condition more common in containers with poor drainage. (See "Containers 101," page 10.)

Feed with citrus fertilizer according to label directions. Don't fret if all of the leaves suddenly drop. Citrus trees often respond to abrupt changes in growing conditions (heat, light, water) in this way. They'll re-leaf. Also note that the fruit take 6 to 12 months to ripen on the tree and don't ripen after picking.

When you spray (and you almost certainly will), favor natural insecticides and fungicides such as *Bacillus subtilis*, *B. thuringiensis*, horticultural oil, insecticidal soap, liquid copper, neem oil, and spinosad. Be aware that citrus plants are also susceptible to root diseases. Use a biological fungicide after harvesting fruit to destroy the fungus or oomycete that causes root rot: Drench the plant until the fungicide solution runs out the bottom of the pot.

If overwintering plants indoors, place the pots in a south-facing window. If they receive less than 6 hours of sunlight per day, use a grow light to supplement natural sunlight. To prevent the plant from drying out, mist the leaves to add humidity. Remember, too, that practically every critter in your yard likes fruit as much as you do. Use netting to foil birds and anchored chicken wire to exclude rabbits.

MY CONTAINER FRUIT

PLANT	PLANTING DATE	OBSERVATIONS

ORNAMENTALS

CONTAINERS, CLOCKWISE FROM
BOTTOM LEFT: WORMWOOD,
SWEET POTATO VINE, PETUNIA,
COLEUS, VERBENA, SWEET POTATO
VINE, CALIBRACHOA

DESIGNING WITH PLANTS

A COLLECTION OF PLANTS IS NOT A LANDSCAPE, ANY MORE THAN A LIST
OF CHOICE WORDS IS A POEM. THE MERIT IS IN THE DESIGN, NOT THE
MATERIAL IT IS EXPRESSED IN, AND THE BEST DESIGNS, LIKE THE BEST
POEMS, MAKE ORDINARY MATERIALS SIGNIFICANT BY THEIR ARRANGEMENT.

–Nancy "Nan" Mary Fairbrother, English writer and lecturer on landscape and land use (1913–71)

For many gardeners, the fun and exciting part of making a container garden is choosing the plants. For some people, though, this is also the hardest part—especially on a stroll through a large nursery, where colors and textures and sizes abound! How do you choose, when you love and want everything?

While there are no hard-and-fast rules for designing a container arrangement—whatever is pleasing to you is perfect—there are still some principles that will help you to understand why some container arrangements are "wows" and some are "woes." Consider these guidelines and then let your imagination run and welcome serendipity.

IMAGINE, IF YOU WILL . . .

A theme, or plan, will give you a baseline on which to build your container arrangement. Think in terms of what you hope to accomplish: Fill space? Add color? Grow food?

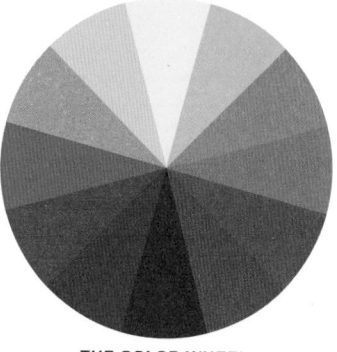

THE COLOR WHEEL

Here are some ideas for creating attractive container arrangements. For more inspiration, try *The Old Farmer's Almanac* Garden Planner software, available for a free 7-day trial at GardenPlanner.Almanac.com.

COLOR

■ A design theme can be based on a common color or a combination of colors.
■ A monochromatic arrangement features one color in a variety of shades (think burgundy, pink, red). Single-color arrangements may look flat.

■ A complementary color scheme features colors found on opposite sides of the color wheel (think green and red, purple and yellow). (See illustration at left.) These can add energy and excitement.
■ Analogous colors are adjacent, or touching each other, on the color wheel (think orange and yellow). These make for a visually calming composition.
■ Bold colors, such as hot pink with orange, introduce drama.
■ Use up to three colors in differing shades and tones. When repeating plants, use odd numbers of them—one, three, five, or seven, depending on the space/size of the container.
■ Blue, violet, and green shades are cool and relaxing to the eye and mind. Red, orange, and yellow shades convey warmth and have been found to encourage activity—even raising people's blood pressure and breathing rates.
■ Purple looks warm when set

AFRICAN LILY (BLUE AND WHITE), SEDGE, AND PETUNIA

CHINESE FRINGE-FLOWER, COLEUS, CORDYLINE, AND NANDINA

next to a cool color and cool when next to a warm color.

■ Use white for contrast and to separate conflicting colors.

■ White and silver are neutral and thus go with everything, as do pale yellow and chartreuse.

■ Repeating a flower color makes for a stronger, more unified arrangement when several containers are placed together.

■ Repeating color in a pattern around the edge of a large container or along the length of a rectangular container (e.g., a window box) lends a sense of rhythm.

■ A riot of numerous colors can seem chaotic, be overwhelming to the eye, and make an arrangement look

busy and out of order.

■ Remember that the color of the container as well as

the environment in which it will reside (on a deck or pool pavement, beside a front door, adjacent to existing bedding plants) also contributes to the appearance of the composition.

DIMENSION

■ Choose a variety of forms. Use tall plants to add height and avoid a flat-looking arrangement and mounded plants to add mass. Allowing cascading or vining plants to drape over the edge of a container "softens" it and adds depth (see sidebar "The Timeless Trio: Thriller, Filler, Spiller," page 97).

■ Use plants that are the proper size in relation to the container and the setting in

PAPYRUS, PENTAS, AND FAIRY FAN-FLOWER

MUKDENIA, AUTUMN FERN, AND HEUCHERA

ELEPHANT EARS, CREEPING JENNY,
DAHLIA, AND LANTANA

PETUNIA, SWEET POTATO VINE, LOBELIA, VERBENA,
PURPLE FOUNTAIN GRASS, AND CREEPING JENNY

which it will be displayed. Plants should be one to two times the height of the visible portion of the container (not including pedestals or other supports).

■ Small plants will be dwarfed by large spaces, and large plants can overpower small spaces.

■ When grouping containers, use at least three of different heights and dimensions to create a layered effect.

■ Ornamental grasses—or any plants that sway in the wind—add a sense of movement.

SHAPE

■ Use plant foliage to your advantage: A variety of leaf shapes and sizes can be more interesting than a collection whose foliage is the same or similar; for instance, combine round-leaf plants with those that have leaves of irregular shape.

■ Consider how each plant will look at maturity—at its full height and shape—and whether all will work together at that scale.

■ Most plants are upright, broad, or trailing. An appealing arrangement usually features at least one of each shape.

TEXTURE

■ Contrasting leaf sizes and textures (aka "surface effect," e.g., hairy, smooth/shiny, rough, leathery) bring interest to an arrangement.

■ Introduce a variety of leaf textures and colors alongside flowering plants (which is called "fusion" gardening). Remember, too, that because foliage will often outlast flowers, it's important to plan for your arrangement to still hold interest after the blooms are gone.

■ Combine three to five species of coarse-, medium-, and fine-texture plants in an arrangement.

ARRANGEMENTS

Here are some classic ways to arrange plants in a container:

■ Identify the "front" of the container, the area that will be most often in view. Place your tallest plant in the back and shorter ones in the front.

■ Sometimes one plant is all that you need. A singularly stunning plant—a "specimen plant"—can be an easy and elegant container display all by itself. A specimen can be an annual, such as elephant ears (which can be overwintered; see page 129); a perennial, such as African blue lily (see page 114); a tropical plant, such as a banana tree (see page 120); or any number of ornamental grasses (see page 132).

■ Put a specimen plant in the center of the container and surround it with annuals or perennials. The specimen serves as the arrangement's anchor and backdrop for the surrounding plants. This is similar to the effect created by a "thriller, filler, spiller" trio.

THE TIMELESS TRIO: THRILLER, FILLER, SPILLER

A popular and winning arrangement that incorporates some of the stated principles use the concept of thriller, filler, spiller:

• A thriller is the captivating focal point plant; it is the vertical element that brings height and drama to the container. This can be a flowering or foliage plant—if flowering, it may have a dramatic bloom; if foliage, it may be bold in leaf shape, texture, or color. As the centerpiece plant, it is usually chosen first.

• Filler plants form the body of the container and serve to hide the stem or stalk of the thriller. They add texture, color, and form to the arrangement and present an opportunity for contrast—for examples, a fine-texture filler would complement a large-leaf thriller, and a round-leaf filler would go well with a spiky thriller.

• Spillers—often vines or trailing plants—anchor the container and spill over its edge to provide a softening effect.

A few thoughts about the arrangement:

• If your container will be fully visible from any side or angle, set your thriller plant in the center of the pot. If the container will be placed against a wall or other structure that restricts full view of it, place the thriller closer to the side of the pot that will abut the wall. This will create the illusion of more space in the container.

• Bear in mind that flowering plants are not always necessary. A trio of vibrant and diverse foliage plants make a stunning arrangement (and often are better suited for shade environments).

• You will find that some of the plants in this book are suggested as thrillers, fillers, and/or spillers. The options are far more numerous than could ever be included here, so have fun trying these and many others!

CLIVIA

Clivia spp.

THOSE INVOLVED WITH GROWING, COLLECTING, AND
BREEDING CLIVIAS ARE OFTEN QUITE INTENSE ABOUT THEIR
PLANTS AND THEIR HOBBY; THEIR INTERESTS SOMETIMES
BORDER ON THE OBSESSIVE. THIS IS NOT UNUSUAL, HOWEVER,
FOR GARDENERS WHO FOCUS ON SPECIFIC PLANT GROUPS
USUALLY WANT ALL OF THE NUANCES AND VARIETIES AVAILABLE
TO THEM. HOWEVER, THE LENGTHS THAT INDIVIDUALS
WILL GO TO GET A SPECIAL CLIVIA ARE SOMETIMES SURPRISING.
–Harold Koopowitz, American writer (b. 1940), in Clivias

The first question that might be asked about clivia is how to pronounce it. Is it KLIV-ee-ah or KLYV-ee-ah? It seems that either is acceptable in most circles, but the story of the plant's origin points to the latter as the preferred articulation: In 1828, John Lindley, a botanist at England's Royal Botanic Gardens, Kew, named the genus to honor Lady Charlotte Clive (rhymes with "dive"), an avid gardener who had cultivated and brought to bloom the first *Clivia nobilis* in England (she may have been the first to do so outside of its native South Africa). First collected by English naturalist William J. Burchell and brought to England in 1815, *C. nobilis* is a pendulous-flower type like many of its cousins. It garnered much attention but fell out of favor following the discovery in the early 1850s of *C. miniata,* with its showier umbel, or cluster, of upright, trumpet-shape, reddish-orange flowers. More than 200 years later, for many people, it's *C. miniata's* spectacular blooms that have the most appeal and make it the most common species grown in the United States today. *C. miniata* does require some special attention in order to be brought to bloom, but many people have done this and you can, too.

A member of the same family (Amaryllidaceae) as amaryllis, clivia shares with its cousin the characteristics of straplike leaves and similarly shaped flowers on a tall stem called a scape (although amaryllis blooms are substantially larger and clivia retains its foliage year-round).

Clivia, also known as bush lily, is a naturally evergreen, shade-loving, herbaceous perennial hardy only in Zones 9 and 10 in the United States. Although it is suitable for in-ground planting, it is vulnerable to frost and thus treated as a houseplant in cold zones. (For more about the African blue lily of the *Agapanthus* genus, see "African Blue Lily," page 114.)

PLANTING

Clivia is propagated by division or seed. Seeds follow the flowers but take up to a year to ripen, during which time they will turn from green to yellow or red, depending on the color of the flower. Harvest seeds once ripe and color has changed. They are slow to germinate (allow several weeks) and mature to bloom in 3 to 5 years. If seeds are unwanted, cut off the fruit after the flowers fall and then remove the scape (stem) at its base after it dries up.

Division is preferred. Mature (3- to 4-year-old) plants usually yield offsets— new plants produced by a mother plant,

WIT & WISDOM

● *Clivia contains the alkaloid lycorine, which is poisonous to pets and people. If eaten, it can cause vomiting and diarrhea. The roots are the most poisonous part. If eaten in large amounts, they can cause convulsions, low blood pressure, tremors, and heart arrhythmias. Nonetheless, clivia was used medicinally by the Zulus to treat fever and snakebite and to relieve pain.*

complete with their own roots—on an annual basis. After the last flower fades, when offsets have three leaves (some growers recommend 9 or 10) at least 8 inches long, remove the plant carefully from the pot (it may be necessary to break a ceramic pot or cut through a plastic one). Brush potting mix from the roots, using a stream of water, if necessary. Identify the offset(s) with roots and separate them from the mother plant by pulling or, if necessary, cutting with a clean, sharp knife. Remove any dead and/or rotting roots. If the offset has been cut off, set it and the mother plant aside overnight or even for a few days (especially if they were hose-soaked) to dry completely before repotting. Keep the bare roots in shade during this time. Plant in equal parts peat moss and coarse sand or perlite and place in a warm spot with moderate (not direct) sunlight. (See "Pondering Peat Moss," page 22.)

Water lightly to moisten but not saturate. Do not allow clivia to rest in standing water, such as in a saucer under the pot—it needs to be dry when resting in winter. Transplant when roots appear on the surface (it is normal for the roots to push up).

In the wild, clivia grows not in soil but in decomposing leaf mold; in the home, it grows best in a light but rich and well-draining potting mix: Use about 50% organic matter (orchid or cactus mix), plus coconut coir or fir bark to aerate the soil. (Roots can rot in heavy, wet soil.)

CARE

Clivia requires lighting that mimics its conditions in the wild: deep or partial shade. In the home, this means bright diffused light such as through a north window or an east or west window shaded from sunlight. Outdoors, this means shade. (Too bright or direct sun can burn the foliage.)

Water regularly, but allow the growing medium to become dry to the touch between waterings. Clivia's fleshy roots store water like a sponge, which enables them to tolerate drought, if necessary. (Overwatering or general wetness can cause root rot.)

Clivia needs a cool, dry period to

VOICES OF EXPERIENCE

My clivia is about 100 years old—really! My husband's parents got it from his grandparents. I got it (after they discarded it in a field) when I was in my 30s, and I'm 73 now. It had a setback 3 years ago when the building that it's kept in had the door blow open during a deep freeze and blowy winter night. The plant was found frozen nearly to the root. It has grown back now and still needs a wheelbarrow to be moved.   –Wendy, via Almanac.com

Mine is a mere baby at 15 years old. It really is wonderful to have it bloom off and on between December and March, despite little care and sitting near a drafty window. It has produced six big offsets, which I have to separate; they are so pot-bound that they are living on air.   –Camille, via Almanac.com

RECOMMENDED VARIETIES

Currently six species are known. *Clivia caulescens, C. gardenii,* and *C. nobilis* are becoming more available, albeit at a price, and breeders continue to produce new hybrids that display the favorable qualities of several species, from flower form and color to leaf variegation.

• *C. caulescens,* aka stalked clivia: grows 2 to 3 feet tall (some reach 6 feet when fully mature); alone among the species in having a thick stalk that produces leaves at the top

• *C. gardenii,* aka Major Garden's clivia (for British Maj. Robert J. Garden, who discovered and collected it in 1855 and sent it to Kew, where it bloomed the next year): slender, tubular, pendulous flowers

• *C. miniata* (the name refers to minium, the color of red lead, and evokes the common flower hue): the only one of the six species that has upright or nearly upright flowers; varieties are available in other colors, as well—near-white, peach, pink, and yellow

• *C. mirabilis* ("miraculous"): discovered in 2002 thriving in full sun in southwestern Africa's Namaqualand

• *C. nobilis:* plant that inspired the genus and whose name suggests nobility; considerably slower grower than other species; from seeds, takes 6 or more years to flower

• *C. robusta:* largest and newest of the species, named in 2004; thrives in marshlands; boasts highest scape at 5 or more feet tall

initiate flowering. In autumn, stop watering and place the plant in a bright, cool (below 50°F) spot for 6 to 12 weeks. (If foliage wilts during this respite, water lightly.) At the conclusion, place clivia in a warmer spot, resume regular watering, and look for flowers in about 8 to 12 weeks.

When the flowers have faded, begin fertilizing monthly, when watering, with a half-strength water-soluble product. Continue until fall, when the plant is brought in for its rest.

Clivia blooms best when it is pot-bound (a clue to this condition would be roots pushing up out of the medium from the base of the plant). Repotting is not immediately required; the plants can go 3 to 5 years in close quarters. However, if you wait too long, clivia will cease flowering. At this point, division is recommended in spring or summer, although any time is fine.

Occasionally, the flower scape (stem) doesn't get tall enough to clear the leaves and the blossoms can't fully open. This can happen for many reasons—too hot, too cold, too bright, too shady, not a long enough chill time—but usually the fertilizer is to blame. Try one with more potassium and phosphorus than nitrogen.

DISEASES/PESTS *(see pages 184–200)*
Diseases: anthracnose, bacterial (Erwinia) soft rot, southern blight. *Pests:* mealy bugs, scale insects, slugs/snails.

FLOWERING MAPLE

Abutilon x *hybridum*

**MAPLES ARE SUCH SOCIABLE TREES. . . .
THEY'RE ALWAYS RUSTLING AND WHISPERING TO YOU.**
–Lucy Maud Montgomery, Canadian writer (1874–1942)

WIT & WISDOM

● *Abutilon's other common names include Chinese lantern, Chinese bellflower, and Indian mallow, although very few species are native to Asia.*

● *Variegation in flowering maple's foliage is caused by Abutilon mosaic virus, which is transmitted in cultivation by grafting or contaminated tools and in nature by the silverleaf whitefly. However, the virus does the plant no harm.*

Pssst! The maple tree in the *Acer* genus of which Montgomery speaks may not tell you that it is not related to the "flowering maple"—perhaps because it wishes it were. Those of the *Abutilon* genus are bountiful bloomers, with leaves that resemble those of the *Acer*, hence the inspiration for its common name. In fact, the flowering maple is a member of the mallow family, which includes hibiscus, hollyhock, okra, and rose of Sharon, and boasts similarly shaped flowers up to 3 inches in diameter that butterflies and hummingbirds love to visit.

We can thank breeders for the beauty and variety in the hundreds of cultivars: It's a houseplant and an outdoor plant. It's compact, at a foot or so tall, or a focal point at several feet. Its three- or five-lobe leaves can be evergreen or variegated. It bears blooms of salmon, orange, red, white, yellow, and bicolors—in some cases, flowers appear in several colors on one plant. Some cultivars bloom in summer and fall, while some more recent hybrids bloom year-round.

Note that leaves can cause minor skin irritation on contact.

Also known as parlor maples, flowering maples are semitropical, frost-tender perennial shrubs winter-hardy in Zones 9 and 10. They can be treated as annuals or overwintered elsewhere and are also suitable for in-ground planting.

PLANTING

Propagation can be by seed or cuttings. Scarify seeds 24 hours before planting (nick or scratch with a fingernail file or sandpaper) to speed germination. Sow on the surface of damp seed-starting mix 8 to 10 weeks before the last frost, barely

RECOMMENDED VARIETIES

● *Abutilon* Bella series: compact (15- to 18-inch) plants; seeds are readily available

● *A.* 'Kristen's Pink': 12 to 16 inches tall; 3-inch-wide, bell-shape flowers

● *A.* 'Souvenir de Bonn': 6 to 10 feet tall; salmon-orange flowers with red veining; leaves edged in creamy white; prune or pinch branches for shorter plant

● *A.* 'Tiger Eye': 6 to 8 feet tall; pendulous yellow flowers with red veining evocative of lanterns; prune or pinch branches for shorter plant

covering them. Maintain the temperature at 75°F and keep the seeds moist. Expect germination in 14 to 21 days.

Softwood tip cuttings can be taken at any time. (Some growers recommend doing so in late summer for the following growing season and, if desired, discarding the parent plant.) Prepare damp seed-starting mix. Dip the 4-inch cutting into rooting hormone and plant. Set aside in a warm, bright room. Provide moderate bottom heat,

SOME FLOWERING MAPLE CULTIVARS BLOOM IN SUMMER AND FALL, WHILE SOME MORE RECENT HYBRIDS BLOOM YEAR-ROUND.

if desired, to speed rooting.

Flowering maples are not picky about soil, but they perform best in rich, well-draining potting mix amended with compost.

Water well and keep constantly moist but not soaking or standing in water.

CARE

Provide full sun to partial shade, depending on the variety.

In spring, pinch the tops of the branches to encourage a compact habit and to avoid legginess. This will also help to keep the plant root-bound and thus control its size—and potentially boost its efflorescence: Plants bloom best when pot-bound. Flowering maples are fast-growing, so repot to a slightly larger container every year or two.

Feed every 2 to 4 weeks, using a fertilizer high in phosphorous—to promote flower production—at half-strength.

For bushier plants, prune occasionally.

If overwintering outdoor plants indoors, provide intense bright light and cool (50° to 60°F) temperatures at night. With sufficient light, many will bloom throughout the winter. Avoid fertilizer and water only enough to keep the soil slightly moist, such as once per month. Note that overwintering can result in a more vigorous plant in the following year.

DISEASES/PESTS *(see pages 184–200)*
Disease: Abutilon mosaic virus (see "Wit & Wisdom"). *Pests:* Those that occur most often on indoor houseplants include aphids, mealy bugs, scale insects, spider mites, and whiteflies.

FUCHSIA

Fuchsia spp.

IN ALL LIKELIHOOD, THE FUCHSIA WILL FALL OUT
OF FASHION LIKE THE WALLFLOWER OR ASTER.

–Oskar Teichert, Silesian gardener (fl. 1858–69), commenting on the overbreeding and excessive publicity and promotion that threatened fuchsia in Europe in the mid-1860s

Fashion fades but style remains, and fuchsia (FEW-shuh) oozes style, with its spectacularly elegant and exotic jewel-tone pendulous flowers that look more like handcrafted silk than nature's handiwork. The plant was discovered in Hispaniola (today, the island of the Dominican Republic and Haiti) and described by French friar and botanist Charles Plumier (1646–1704) in the 1690s. He chose the genus name to honor 16th-century German botanist Leonhard Fuchs (pronounced "fooks"; 1501–66). However, this semitropical to tropical gem was not cultivated and propagated in Europe for nearly a century: In 1788, fuchsia was introduced to England's Royal Botanic Gardens, Kew, where a nurseryman was able to reproduce several hundred plants from cuttings. In ensuing years, new species and varieties were discovered, hybridized, and multiplied by botanists and growers across Europe. As they shared their plant stocks and knowledge in colorful catalogs, the demand for ever-different forms and flower hues for public gardens and private properties exploded, inspiring Teichert's observation under the opening photo.

Today, more than 100 species are known, and thousands of cultivars have been developed (although not all of these may be available or easily acquired). A member of the evening primrose family (Onagraceae), fuchsia

RECOMMENDED VARIETIES

Annuals
• *Fuchsia* 'Aurea': the most commonly grown; prostrate, upright, trailing habits; 3 to 5 feet tall and/or wide; many color combinations

• *F.* 'Southgate': semi-trailing habit; 4 to 8 inches tall, 18 to 24 inches wide; medium-size, double, light pink, bicolor flowers

• *F.* 'Swingtime': trailing habit; 1 to 2 feet tall, 18 to 30 inches wide; large, double, scarlet and white flowers

Half-Hardy
• *F.* 'Dark Eyes': upright shrub form; 1 to 2 feet tall, 24 to 30 inches wide; medium-size, double, red and violet-blue flowers

• *F.* 'Roesse Blacky': shrub form with a lax and arching habit; 1 foot tall, 1 to 2 feet wide; medium-size, semidouble, red and dark purple to black flowers

Half-Hardy to Hardy
• *F.* 'Cardinal': upright shrub; 3 to 6 feet tall, 3 to 4 feet wide; magenta and red flowers

• *F.* 'Margaret': shrub; 4 feet tall and wide; fast-growing; used as a hedge; semidouble red and violet flowers

Hardy
• *F.* 'Prince of Orange': bush hybrid; 2 feet tall and wide; pale orange to red-orange flowers

• *F.* 'Remembrance': shrub hybrid; 3 to 4 feet tall and wide; pale pink and red flowers

WIT & WISDOM

● *The berries produced after fuchsia flowers fade can be eaten or prepared as sauces and jams and in baked goods. They are best when soft and squishy; the flavor runs from peppery to lemony. Single-flower plants (not double- or semidouble-) usually produce more fruit because less of their energy goes into the flowers.*

● *Although California fuchsia, native to that state, has a red flower that resembles those of some* Fuchsia *species, it in fact is the species* Epilobium canum.

● F. excorticata *produces blue pollen, which at one time was used by Māori women in New Zealand to adorn their faces.*

is native to Central and South America; three species, including a tree form, are indigenous to New Zealand. Hummingbirds find fuchsias irresistible.

Fuchsias' hardiness varies: Some are tender in Zones 10 and 11; some are half-hardy and tolerate conditions in Zones 9 and 10; some are hardy enough (to Zone 6 or 7, or –10° to 0°F) to be grown in-ground, if protected from harsh winter weather.

Fuchsia is a tender perennial, flowering from late spring to first frost; except as indicated above, it is grown as an annual in most areas of North America.

TODAY, MORE THAN 100 SPECIES ARE KNOWN, AND THOUSANDS OF FUCHSIA CULTIVARS HAVE BEEN DEVELOPED.

PLANTING

Fuchsia can be grown from seeds or stem tip cuttings; the latter is the easier method, as the former can take up to 4 months. Cuttings can be taken in spring (before flowers appear) or fall (these plants tend to bloom sooner than spring-rooted ones). Prepare containers with seed-starting mix or use equal parts sand, perlite, and peat moss; moisten the medium. (See "Pondering Peat Moss," page 22.) Cut off a green branch that is up to 6 inches long and has three pairs

of leaves. Remove the bottom pair and dip the cut end into rooting hormone (if using; not necessary). Insert the cutting into the medium up to the next leaves. Cover loosely with clear plastic and set in a warm, bright spot out of direct sun. Fall-rooted cuttings do not need a cover and prefer a cool (45° to 50°F), bright environment. Water enough to prevent wilting; avoid getting the leaves wet. When new leaf growth appears (in 3 to 4 weeks), lift the seedling and transplant it to a container. Most fuchsias need space to grow. Provide an 8- to 10-inch pot, depending on variety.

Prepare a light, airy, well-draining potting mix. Add pelletized, slow-release fertilizer to the medium (according to the package directions).

Shelter the plant for about 10 days before gradually introducing it to the outdoors when all danger of frost in your area has passed or daytime temperatures are consistently above 50°F.

CARE

Water when the surface of the growing medium is dry. Plants like roots moist but not soggy. During warm and/or dry spells, mist leaves.

In spring (March or April), fertilize with a half-strength balanced solution weekly. If desired, apply a "bloom formula" (ideally, with a small amount of nitrogen) when plants are setting buds.

Fuchsia flowers on new growth, so pinch back, or deadhead, faded blooms. (If flowers fail to form, prune to the

FUCHSIA FLOWERS ON NEW GROWTH, SO PINCH BACK, OR DEADHEAD, FADED BLOOMS.

first strong node.) In spring, pinch back to one set of leaves after two sets have formed to encourage bushiness.

Fuchsias need long days to flower. Most thrive in partial to full shade and where moderate humidity and temperatures (below 85°F) prevail. In hot environments, morning sun and afternoon shade are advised. Extreme summer heat and/or dry conditions can cause flower buds—and ultimately the plant—to fail.

Where winter brings cold, withhold fertilizer in the fall to prepare the plant for dormancy.

If overwintering a hanging basket, prune trailing stems to the side of the container and top growth to no less than 3 inches. Remove the plant from the pot. Examine the root ball; if pests are present, apply insecticidal soap to the plant and roots. Wash and rinse the pot. Repot, adding some organic potting mix. Lightly water (do not fertilize) to dampen roots. Store the plant in a cool (40° to 45°F minimum) place that will not freeze but has good air circulation. Low, indirect light is fine but not necessary. Lay the pot on its side (this encourages root growth). Water about once per month, rotating the pot one-quarter turn each time to balance root growth.

In spring (March), place the plant in partial sun, start watering again, and reintroduce diluted fertilizer. Repot if desired or necessary.

DISEASES/PESTS (see pages 184–200) *Diseases:* Phytophthora crown and root rot, rust. *Pests:* aphids, fuchsia gall mites, mealy bugs, scale insects, spider mites, thrips, whiteflies.

PALM-LEAF BEGONIA

Begonia luxurians

AND SOME CAN POT BEGONIAS AND SOME CAN BUD A ROSE, AND SOME ARE HARDLY FIT TO TRUST WITH ANYTHING THAT GROWS.
–Rudyard Kipling, English writer (1865–1936), in "The Glory of the Garden"

Resembling a delicate palm tree, palm-leaf begonia has an upright, cane-stem form with 8- to 15-finger, draping palmate leaves that are green with reddish copper undersides. It is native to the Brazilian rain forest, where it thrives in the understory—which explains some of its special needs. When grown outdoors, palm-leaf begonia can reach to 13 feet tall; indoors, a 6-foot height is more likely, although the larger the pot, the higher the plant, if optimum conditions are maintained. Fragrant, cream-color flower clusters appear from late winter into summer when grown outdoors; blooms are not assured indoors. It is a sensation alone or with other plants.

Palm-leaf begonia is a frost-tender, evergreen perennial winter-hardy in Zones 10 and 11 and overwintered indoors elsewhere.

PLANTING

The best time to pot or repot is early spring.

Purchasing a plant is an option, although palm-leaf begonia propagates easily: Place a shoot (tip cutting) with several leaves in a small jar of water. (The plant releases root hormones, so using

WIT & WISDOM

- *The genus was named for Frenchman Michel Bégon (1638–1710), a plant collector and patron of botany, by his French Franciscan monk friend, botanist Charles Plumier (1646–1704).*

- Solution solution: *To discourage powdery mildew, treat plants seasonally with a preventative spray made from 1 tablespoon baking soda, 1 tablespoon vegetable oil, and ½ teaspoon liquid dish soap in 1 gallon of water.*

a relatively small amount of water will prevent them from becoming diluted.) If the stem cutting remains firm, even if foliage falls, it should produce roots. When three or more half-inch roots appear, plant in moist, not saturated, potting mix amended with compost.

Use tepid water to maintain moisture (the roots are sensitive).

CARE

Provide diffuse, or filtered, light from an eastern or western exposure. Avoid the midday sun, as well as too much darkness, which can result in mold on the soil and/or root rot.

Palm-leaf begonia performs best when humidity levels are 50% or more (lower levels can be tolerated for short periods); regular misting or a tray of shallow water under the pot can help in dry environments. (Be aware that yellow halos on brown leaf tips are a sign of too-low humidity.)

Allow the plant to dry out between waterings, then add tepid water until some runs out of the bottom of the pot.

Fertilize with a balanced formula every 2 weeks during active growing periods (reduce frequency in winter). When the plant is budding or in bloom, fertilize

with a formula that is high in potassium to prolong the flowering period.

Every 10 to 14 days, wipe the topsides of the leaves with a damp towel to keep them clean.

Pinch the tips to encourage branching; prune at any time when growth is excessive.

Indoors, keep in a temperature of at least 60°F.

To maintain size, prune (as much as a third) after flowering or whenever growth is excessive or leggy. (Propagate the cuttings.)

Repot in spring; soak roots before moving to minimize damage to them. Allow 1 month to pass before fertilizing a newly potted palm-leaf begonia.

Failure to flower outdoors can be the result of insufficient dormancy. To address, lower the ambient temperature in autumn and winter, reduce watering, and eliminate fertilizer.

DISEASES/PESTS *(see pages 184–200)*
Diseases: powdery mildew, Pythium root and stem rot, Rhizoctonia root and stem rot. *Pests:* none serious; sometimes spider mites.

RECOMMENDED VARIETIES
This is a singular species.

TREE IVY

x Fatshedera lizei

**THE TREE WHICH MOVES SOME TO TEARS OF JOY IS IN
THE EYES OF OTHERS ONLY A GREEN THING THAT STANDS IN
THE WAY. SOME SEE NATURE ALL RIDICULE AND DEFORMITY,
AND SCARCE SEE NATURE AT ALL. BUT TO THE EYES OF THE MAN
WITH IMAGINATION, NATURE IS IMAGINATION ITSELF.**
–William Blake, English poet (1757–1827)

Cry for joy! This "green thing," tree ivy, is a bush or a tree—or whatever you want it to be! Produced in 1910 at the Lize Frères (Lize Brothers) Nursery in Nantes, France, this eye-catching specimen is a cross between shrubby Moser's Japanese fatsia (*Fatsia japonica* 'Moseri') and a common climbing English ivy *(Hedera helix)*. Both plants are in the family Araliaceae but belong to different genera—and this is what makes the specimen special. (Most hybrids are instead crosses within the same genus.) This unique pairing of *Fatsia* and *Hedera* produces a 3- to 5-foot-tall, bushy evergreen with an irregular mounding habit and trailing stems when pinched and pruned accordingly. If trained to stand tall and supported, the tree form can reach 10 feet in height. (Uncontrolled, this marvel will form an irregular, sprawling mass.)

On the way up, tree ivy will climb, but—unlike its ivy parent—it will not cling to inside or outside walls. Yes, it's a patio plant or a houseplant, and this is not all. Tree ivy thrives in dappled or full shade; direct sun will burn its

'ANGYO STAR' GROWS UP TO 6 FEET TALL AND 4 TO 5 FEET WIDE.

giant (4- to 8-inch-wide) glossy green, five-lobe leaves. On rare occasion, umbels of white flowers may appear in autumn—but so seldom as to be deemed insignificant. The plant tolerates air pollution and salt spray and, with proper care, can last 40 years or more.

Also known as aralia ivy or botanical wonder, tree ivy is a perennial, semi-hardwood, evergreen hardy in Zones 7 to 11 and/or to 10°F (colder temperatures may cause severe dieback, but regrowth from the roots should occur); elsewhere,

WIT & WISDOM

● Fatsia japonica, *the species of one of tree ivy's parent plants, originated in Japan. The name "fatsia" is the Latinization of the Japanese word* fatsi, *meaning "eight" in reference to the plant leaf's eight lobes. (The plant is known as* yatsude, *meaning "eight fingers," in Japan.)*

● *English ivy* (Hedera helix, *which has come to mean the clinging plant that coils in spirals) has a deep cultural history: Ancient Greeks and Romans believed that wearing a wreath of ivy leaves on the head would prevent the wearer from becoming inebriated. They also valued ivy as a symbol of achievement, so ivy wreaths were often awarded to recognized athletes and intellectuals.*

it welcomes overwintering. It is also suitable for in-ground growing.

PLANTING

Tree ivy is sterile, so it can not be grown from seeds. Purchase a plant or propagate it from a cutting about 6 inches long. Prepare a pot of damp potting mix. Remove any foliage from the lower (cut) half of the cutting and dip it into rooting hormone. Plant the cutting and place it in a warm spot that gets indirect light. Keep the medium moist but not soaking. (Some advise placing it in a plastic bag.) When growth is apparent at the tips or the cutting resists a light tug, transplant it to a larger pot filled with potting mix.

Tree ivy thrives in well-draining potting mix amended with compost.

Provide even moisture but avoid soggy soil, which can cause root rot.

CARE

Place the plant in dappled sunlight, light shade, or full shade.

Maintain moisture but not to excess.

A balanced fertilizer (such as for houseplants) applied according to package directions can be used in summer. No fertilizer is advised in winter.

Pinch or prune at any time to maintain bushiness. (It can be pruned back hard to be returned to small shrub form.) If height is desired, train and provide support.

Hardiness to 5°F has been reported, but this could cause dieback. Bring indoors to overwinter; the plant will brighten a shadowy room. Place tree ivy in low light to semi-darkness—for example, in an area with northern window exposure in a hallway or near a staircase or the like—ideally, in a 50° to 70°F environment. Water less frequently. Until spring, avoid fertilizing.

To rejuvenate a plant that has experienced dieback or if you want to start anew, prune or cut back to retain about 2 feet of the main stalk. If stem cuttings are suitable, use them to propagate new plants.

DISEASES/PESTS *(see pages 184–200)* *Diseases:* anthracnose, bacterial leaf spot, fungal leaf spot, Rhizoctonia root and stem rot. *Pests:* aphids, mealy bugs, scale insects, spider mites.

RECOMMENDED VARIETIES

The only species is x *Fatshedera lizei*. Variegated cultivars that have come from it include . . .

• x *F. lizei* 'Angyo Star': up to 6 feet tall, 4 to 5 feet wide; splotches of creamy white variegation on leaves

• x *F. lizei* 'Annemieke', aka 'Anna Mikkels', 'Aureamaculata', and 'Lemon Lime': 3 to 5 feet tall and wide; variegated leaves feature yellow splashes in the center

• x *F. lizei* 'Curly': up to 3 feet tall, 4 to 6 feet wide; edges of dark green foliage "twist," or curl, hence its name; burgundy stems

• x *F. lizei* 'Variegata': up to 4 to 6 feet tall, up to 10 feet wide; leaves have cream-color margins

AFRICAN BLUE LILY

Agapanthus spp.

**IT IS A LONG TIME SINCE MY LAST VISIT. . . .
I MUST SAY, YOUR AGAPANTHUS ARE FLOURISHING.**
–*Albus Dumbledore to Vernon Dursley, husband of Harry's Aunt Petunia in* Harry Potter
and the Half-Blood Prince *by J. K. Rowling, English writer (b. 1965)*

I t'll cast a spell on you. True to its name, agapanthus—known in ancient Greece as love flower (*agape* means "love"; *anthos*, "flower")—tends to leave owners and observers besotted with its beauty. From a base of straplike leaves, sturdy stems (scapes) rise above its foliage to terminate in umbels (clusters) of up to 100 lilylike flowers in shades of blue, purple, or white. Its common names of African blue lily (*Agapanthus africanus*) and lily of the Nile hint at its origin, but only one is accurate: Agapanthus is native to South Africa, not the Nile basin; the reason for the river moniker is a mystery. Note, too, that this plant is not in the lily family, although years ago it was indeed included there. Today, it is the only genus in Agapanthoideae, a subfamily of the Amaryllidaceae family, which itself also includes clivia (see page 98).

Hybridizing has resulted in more than 600 varieties with many differences beyond their apparent similarities: Depending on the variety and species, agapanthus can be evergreen or deciduous; have stems that rise from several inches to multiple feet tall; and bear funnel-, bell-, trumpet-, or tubular-form flowers that vary in their bloom periods.

Evergreen types retain their foliage and in winter should be treated like houseplants (provided with water and bright light in a 55° to 60°F environment); deciduous ones lose their strapping leaves in winter but can be stored in a cool (40° to 50°F), dark, frost-free space in their pot or wrapped in newspaper with their soil removed after they have been lifted. If somewhat pot-bound, agapanthus tends to flower abundantly. Dwarf forms are especially suited to being grown in containers.

Agapanthus is a tender perennial hardy in Zones 7/8 to 11; plants may be overwintered or treated as annuals elsewhere. Its cut flowers last up to 10 days.

RECOMMENDED VARIETIES

Evergreen species (*Agapanthus africanus, A. praecox*) include the following; consult your nursery for others.

- *A. africanus* 'Albus': white flowers; 2 to 4 feet tall; provide partial sun/filtered light

- *A. africanus* 'Peter Pan': blue flowers; 1 to 2 feet tall; provide partial sun/filtered light

- *A.* 'Ever Sapphire': deep blue flowers; 1 to 2 feet tall; provide partial sun/filtered light

- *A. praecox* 'Flore Pleno': deep, lavender blue double flowers; 2 to 3 feet tall; provide partial sun/filtered light

- *A.* 'Queen Anne': blue flowers; 1 to 2 feet tall; provide partial sun/filtered light

- *A.* 'Snow Storm': white flowers; 2 to 3 feet tall; provide partial sun/filtered light

- *A.* 'Snowball': white flowers; 1 to 2 feet tall; provide partial sun/filtered light

Note: Deciduous species are seldom available as ornamentals.

PLANTING

Purchasing an agapanthus plant is advised as a start; dividing one later can result in more plants. When starting from seeds, sow them ¼ inch deep in potting mix in spring and allow 1 month or more for germination. Soaking seeds in water for 24 hours may speed up germination. Plants started from seeds will take 2 to 5 years to flower.

Use a well-draining, loam-based compost mix or potting mix in containers. Plants do not tolerate excess water.

Plant a rhizome 1 inch deep in a container 8 to 12 inches in diameter; water well.

AGAPANTHUS IS A TENDER PERENNIAL HARDY IN ZONES 7/8 TO 11.

CARE

Provide at least 6 hours of direct sun.

Water regularly but avoid overwatering.

Fertilize lightly twice a year (spring and midsummer) with a high-potassium formula. Excess fertilization can result in lanky growth.

In zones that do not freeze, cut the stems when flowers pass but leave the foliage. If uncut, flowers will develop and drop seeds. Remove any dead foliage from deciduous types before bringing them indoors for the winter.

Divide root-bound potted plants every 4 to 5 years; divide evergreen varieties immediately after flowering and deciduous ones in spring before growth starts. With a sharp knife, cut the rhizome clump into sections, making sure that each division has at least a couple of growing points and roots attached. Pot them. Allow a year or more for divisions to flower. Note that failure to divide a severely pot-bound plant can hinder flowering.

DISEASES/PESTS (see pages 184–200)

Disease: Botrytis blight. *Pests:* mealy bugs, slugs/snails, spider mites, thrips.

WIT & WISDOM

● *In its place of origin, agapanthus is considered both medicinal and magical. It is used for numerous ailments, from the common cold to heart disease, and its leaves are used as bandages.*

● *For some people, agapanthus sap can cause minor skin irritation or dermatitis and severe mouth pain if ingested.*

● *Occasionally, a blue-flowering agapanthus may produce white blooms. It is not known why this happens, but such a plant seldom reverts to producing blue flowers.*

AGAVE

Agave spp.

TODAY I SPROUTED A BIG GREEN STALK
LIKE A STEEPLE POINTING HIGH
INCH BY INCH, FLOWER BY FLOWER
I GROW UNTIL I REACH THE SKY.
WHEN I REACH MY GREATEST HEIGHT
I JUST CAN'T TAKE IT ANYMORE
MY ROOTS BREAK AND THEN LET GO . . .
AND I TOPPLE TO THE DESERT FLOOR.
WITHOUT ROOTS, I WILL DIE
BUT THIS IS THE WAY IT SHOULD BE
ON MY STALK THERE ARE MANY SEEDS
TO MAKE A BRAND-NEW ME!

–"Octopus Agave" by Matthew Zamora, third grader and overall winner (in a tie)
in 2008 Earth Day Poetry Contest, Arizona-Sonora Desert Museum, Tucson, Arizona

RECOMMENDED VARIETIES

• *Agave americana* 'Variegata': hardy in Zones 8 to 11; 5 to 8 feet tall, 10 to 15 feet wide; the name refers to the color of its blue-gray leaves, which have yellow edges in a rosette growth pattern; produces yellow-green flowers; pups emerge from the base

• *A. attenuata,* aka foxtail agave: hardy in Zones 10 and 11; 2 to 3 feet tall, 3 to 6 feet wide; pale blue to yellow-green spineless leaves; the name refers to its arching stalk 10 or more feet long, on which form rosettes that eventually turn into thousands of yellow-green flowers

• *A. lophantha* 'Quadricolor': hardy in Zones 8 to 10; 12 to 18 inches tall, up to 2 feet wide; the name refers to the hues of its red-tooth leaves, which have dark green centers, pale green stripes, and yellow edges; in cold temperatures, leaves turn pink to red; produces yellow flowers; offsets can be taken in spring or autumn

• *A. ovatifolia,* aka whale's tongue agave: hardy in Zones 7 to 11; 3 to 4 feet tall, 4 to 6 feet wide; name describes the rosette of slightly cupped, powdery blue to gray leaves with small teeth; produces yellow-green flowers on 14-foot stalk after 10 years; reproduces by seed and bulbils

• *A. parryi,* aka Parry's agave: hardy in Zones 7 to 10; 1 to 3 feet tall, 1 to 3 feet wide; slate-gray/blue foliage forms a tight whirling rosette of toothed leaves; produces yellow flowers on 10- to 20-foot-tall stalks; offsets grow from the base

• *A. vilmoriniana,* aka octopus agave: hardy in Zones 9 to 11; 3 to 4 feet tall, 5 to 6 feet wide; toothless, gray-green, undulating leaves resemble octopi tentacles; produces golden yellow flowers on 10- to 20-foot stalk; plantlets form along the bloom mast

Agave is a long-lived denizen of the desert whose stunningly exotic species number more than 200. Its flowers bloom anytime from their 6th to 30th year—and indicate that the plant's end is near: The mast (or stalk or stem) rises, the flowers bloom, and, in most cases, the plant then dies. (Plants that go through this process are termed "monocarpic.") At this point, next-generational offshoots, aka "pups," can be replanted to start the growing cycle anew. Agave, native variously to Mexico and the southwestern United States and often mistaken for yucca, produces twisting, speared, splayed, and spiking leaves that set a spectacular scene. After becoming established, agaves thrive on neglect. Wear protective gloves when handling agave and be aware that because its leaf tips are mildly toxic, they should be cut off in landscapes frequented by children. One agave in a pot can be a showstopper.

Agaves are evergreen perennials winter-hardy in Zones 5 to 11, depending on cultivar; they can be treated as annuals or overwintered elsewhere.

PLANTING

Choose an unglazed pot, if possible, to allow for evaporation of excess moisture.

Provide a container mixture made from equal parts potting mix, compost, and gravel, pumice, or sand. Alternately, plant in cactus mix.

AFTER BECOMING ESTABLISHED, AGAVES THRIVE ON NEGLECT.

Agaves, being succulents, have shallow root systems. Remove a plant from the store pot, brush the soil from its root system, and open the roots. Position the plant's crown to sit well above the soil line and remain there after the soil settles.

Water once or twice a week during the first month.

CARE

Agave thrives in full sun but can tolerate some late afternoon shade.

Water once a week during the hottest part of the summer and less so during cool seasons. Allow soil to dry out by at least half between waterings.

In spring, apply a light dose of balanced, granular, slow-release fertilizer, if desired. Note that fertilizer may encourage blooming, which will result in the plant's demise.

Repot every year or so to replenish the soil and enable root-pruning. Although agaves are shallow-rooted, the size of a container should complement the scale of its plant.

DISEASES/PESTS (see pages 184–200)

Diseases: anthracnose, crown rot (of agave). *Pests:* agave snout weevil; sometimes agave plant bugs (aka running bugs), eriophyid mites, scale insects.

WIT & WISDOM

- *The name "agave" comes from the Greek* agavos, *meaning "illustrious" or "admirable."*
- *American agave,* A. americana, *is one of the agave species sometimes known by the common name "century plant." This misnomer stems from a previous (inaccurate) belief that the plant bloomed only after 100 years had passed.*

BANANA

Musa spp. and other genera

AN OLD BANANA LEAF WAS ONCE YOUNG AND GREEN.
–Nigerian proverb

ere are plants with "a-peel"! Some 50 different species of bananas are available, some ornamental and some producing edible fruit. With luxurious foliage, an elegant profile, and a larger-than-life impact, a banana plant in a container lends a tropical air to any setting—a pool, patio, pond, or property.

PLANTING

The most important consideration may be the container. Think big, and then think bigger: While a banana plant may be started in a 1-gallon pot, a mature one may do best in a 15- to 25-gallon container.

Purchasing a banana plant is advised. Propagation is usually by suckers (aka "pups").

Avoid exposing the plant to temperatures below 60°F, as growth will stop at 50°F and the threat of injury will increase. Plant outdoors 3 to 4 weeks after last frost.

RECOMMENDED VARIETIES

• *Ensete ventricosum* 'Maurelii', aka red/Abyssinian/wild banana: a fast-growing ornamental plant, similar to those in the *Musa* genus; winter-hardy in Zones 10 and 11, overwinter indoors elsewhere; grows 8 to 10 feet tall in temperate regions, with maroon-red tints on paddle-like foliage and leaf axils; white flowers, usually after 3 to 5 years (although not on those cut close to the soil for overwintering); fruit is inedible

• *Musa acuminata* 'Dwarf Cavendish', aka Chinese/ladyfinger banana: winter-hardy in Zones 9 to 11, overwinter indoors elsewhere; grows 4 to 8 feet tall, with paddle-shape green leaves; cream to yellow flowers, usually in year 2 or 3 (although not on those cut close to the soil for overwintering); fruit is edible but seldom appears on overwintered plants

• *M. acuminata* 'Dwarf Orinoco': winter-hardy in Zones 7 to 11, overwinter indoors elsewhere; grows vigorously to 5 to 6 feet tall, with large, paddle-shape foliage; pink flowers may appear on mature plants (although not on those cut close to the soil for overwintering); fruit is edible but seldom appears on overwintered plants

• *M. basjoo*, aka Japanese (fiber) banana: an ornamental plant; winter-hardy in Zones 9 and 10, overwinter indoors elsewhere; grows 6 to 14 feet tall, with paddle-shape green leaves up to 6 feet long and 2 feet wide; cream-to-yellow flowers may appear on mature plants (although not on those cut close to the soil for overwintering); fruit is inedible

• *M.* 'Siam Ruby': an ornamental plant; winter-hardy in Zones 9 to 11, overwinter indoors elsewhere; compact habit, grows up to 8 feet tall; foliage and pseudostems are dark maroon red, with spots/streaks of chartreuse; provide full sun for deepest red color; plant may produce tubular, cream-color flowers, although seldomly; fruit is inedible

• *M. velutina*, aka pink/hairy banana: winter-hardy in Zones 7b to 11, overwinter indoors elsewhere; grows 4 to 6 feet tall, with paddle-shape, dark green foliage; cream/yellow/pink flowers may appear (although not on those cut close to the soil for overwintering); peels are pink; flesh is white and edible but heavily seeded

• *Musella lasiocarpa*, aka Chinese dwarf/golden lotus banana: an ornamental plant; winter-hardy in Zones 7 to 10, overwinter indoors elsewhere; grows 3 to 6 feet tall, with 1- to 4-foot-long, gray-green leaves; prized for its yellow flowers (usually in its second year, then annually); fruit that follows the inflorescence (especially in warm zones) is inedible

WIT & WISDOM

• *A banana plant is a large herb that rises on a pseudostem, a thick cylinder of overlapping, tightly packed leaf sheaths that rise from its fibrous root system. It is not a tree, with a stem or trunk.*

• *When the pink bananas of* Musa velutina *are ripe, their peels will open by themselves to reveal the white flesh inside.*

Banana plants are very heavy feeders. Use a slow-release fertilizer when planting or repotting. Provide well-draining, fertile potting mix amended with compost and/or aged manure as needed that is slightly acidic, with a pH of 5.5 to 6.5.

Water thoroughly when planting or transplanting.

CARE

Provide full sun but be prepared to provide partial shade or filtered sun in the heat of the day.

Protect the foliage from winds that may lead to leaf damage.

Water regularly with 1 to 2 inches per week or more. Keep soil consistently moist but not saturated; do not allow to dry out. Persistent drought will cause leaf burn.

Fertilize regularly with a balanced, slow-release formula.

Prepare to overwinter before the first fall frost by either bringing the potted plant into a large, sunny room and then reducing its water and fertilization or else cutting off the potted plant's foliage before storing it in a cool, dark, frost-free area (for ease in handling, the plant can also be cut back close to the soil). Provide it with an occasional light watering. If the plant and container are too large to move, trim off the foliage, remove the plant, wrap the roots in plastic, and then store in the basement or garage as above—but avoid watering.

DISEASES/PESTS *(see pages 184–200)*
Diseases: anthracnose, black Sigatoka disease, Panama disease, southern bacterial wilt (aka "Moko disease"), viruses (including cucumber mosaic virus). *Pests:* aphids, mealy bugs, scale insects, spider mites. In addition to these threats, outdoor plants are also susceptible to banana weevils and root-knot nematodes.

'DWARF CAVENDISH' HAS DISTINCTIVE PADDLE-SHAPE GREEN LEAVES.

CANNA

Canna spp.

**FROM THE TALL CANNA'S SABLE POLISH'D SEEDS
THE PIOUS NUN PREPARES HER HOLY BEADS . . .**
–Frances Arabella Rowden, English poet (c. 1774–1820),
in A Poetical Introduction to the Study of Botany

123

Although often referred to as "bulbs," cannas are not true bulbs; they multiply beneath the soil by way of "rhizomes," which are modified stems that grow horizontally. Similarly, even though they are commonly referred to as "lilies," this is not accurate either. However, cannas can truly be thrillers, as their paddle-shape leaves in shades of green, bronze, or burgundy—and perhaps with stripes or variegation—wrap around stems that bear large but delicate, gladiolus-like flowers of red, pink, orange, and yellow that keep coming from late spring or early summer to first frost. When most flowers can't take the heat of late July and early August, cannas thrive. Standing knee-high to over 8 feet tall, depending on the cultivar, cannas in containers can thrill as one plant looking spectacular as a focal point, as several in a row grandly delineating a border, and/or as a clustered group adding depth to a narrow area.

Also known as Indian shot, canna is a sun-loving tropical or subtropical herbaceous perennial hardy in Zones 7 to 10 and treated as an annual to be lifted and stored elsewhere.

PLANTING

Cannas are propagated by division in spring (every 3 or 4 years) or from seeds. Start seeds (preferably from the Tropical or South Pacific series) indoors in February. Scarify (nick or scratch with a fingernail file or sandpaper) to expose the light-color interior. Soak in water for 24 hours, then plant in and cover lightly with a seed-starting medium. Water, allow to drain, then cover with plastic wrap. Maintain at 70° to 75°F. After germination occurs, in 7 to 14 days, remove the plastic and place in sunlight or under fluorescent lights. When seedlings are large enough to handle, transplant them to large containers—at least 18 inches in diameter—and continue to provide light and moisture. Plant in potting mix amended with aged manure or compost and add a slow-release fertilizer. Harden off before moving outdoors permanently after all danger of frost has passed. (Note that seeds can be stored dry, at room temperature, for years.)

WIT & WISDOM

- *The genus name comes from the Greek* kanna, *meaning "reed."*
- *Canna flowers attract butterflies and hummingbirds.*
- *Canna seeds, being perfectly round and hard like BB pellets, have been used in jewelry, prayer beads, and baby rattles.*
- *Canna has been cultivated as a food crop in Central and South America for thousands of years. The rhizomes are edible; the foliage is used as animal fodder when feed is scarce.*

Canna rhizomes are heavy feeders that perform best in rich, organic potting mix amended with aged manure or compost, although they may tolerate poor soil. The soil must be well-draining; rhizomes can tolerate brief drought but risk rotting in wet soil.

Plant rhizomes 4 to 6 inches deep to receive full sun for 6 to 8 hours per day.

Water well and abundantly.

CARE

Water regularly to maintain evenly moist soil.

During the growing season, fertilize monthly with a balanced (10-10-10) formula.

Remove spent blooms to encourage more and tidy the plant.

In fall, after the first frost, cut stems to about 1 to 3 inches long.

Rhizomes in containers can be overwintered in a dark basement or garage where the temperature remains above 40°F. However, lifting from the container is recommended. Shake off the growing medium and set into a container along with peat moss or vermiculite. (See "Pondering Peat Moss," page 22.) Spray the rhizomes with water occasionally to avoid root shriveling. Note that some varieties overwinter better than others.

DISEASES/PESTS *(see pages 184–200)*
Diseases: aster yellows, bacterial bud rot, Botrytis blight, fungal leaf spot, rust, viruses (including bean yellow mosaic virus, canna yellow mottle virus).
Pests: canna leaf rollers (larger and lesser), Japanese beetles, root-knot nematodes, slugs/snails, spider mites.

RECOMMENDED VARIETIES

• Canna 'City of Portland': 4 to 5 feet tall; green foliage with coral-pink flowers

• *C.* x *ehemanii*, aka Ehemann's canna: 5 to 8 feet tall; green foliage with deep rose-pink flowers

• *C. indica* 'Pretoria', aka Bengal Tiger: 4 to 6 feet tall; variegated yellow-and-green striped foliage with orange flowers

• *C.* x *generalis* 'Futurity Red': 2 to 4 feet tall, on average; burgundy foliage with crimson flowers; self-cleaning (drops spent flowers)

• *C.* x *generalis* 'Phasion', aka Tropicanna: 5 to 6 feet tall; burgundy foliage that develops green, pink, red, and yellow stripes; bright orange flowers

• *C.* 'Musifolia', aka banana canna: 8 to 10 feet tall; dark green foliage with red veining and stems; orange-red flowers

• *C.* 'Toucan Yellow': 2½ to 4 feet tall; deep green foliage with golden-yellow flowers

CORDYLINE

Cordyline spp.

**THE TIME HAS COME, THE WALRUS SAID, TO TALK
OF MANY THINGS: OF SHOES—AND SHIPS—
AND SEALING WAX—OF CABBAGES AND KINGS.**
–Lewis Carroll, English writer (1832–98), in Through the Looking Glass

Legend has it that *Cordyline australis* was given one of its common names, cabbage tree, by British naval explorer James Cook while visiting New Zealand (the plant's native habitat) because he found its edible foliage to be a suitable substitute for that vegetable. Its cousin, *C. fruticosa* (formerly *C. terminalis),* aka the good luck plant or Ti plant, charmed early Polynesians into thinking that it had magical powers and that its presence could protect members of a household from evil spirits. As the King of Tropical Foliage plant, cordyline brings majestic, exotic flair to almost any setting.

With spiky, sometimes daggerlike, foliage, cordylines present distinctly different profiles; many landscape designers call them architectural plants. Among the 15 species and many more varieties, the plants bear distinctive leaf shapes, sizes, and colors: Foliage shades range from pink, red, purple, and green to orange and white, often in combinations. The most common species among home gardeners is *C. fruticosa*, which in temperate zones typically winters indoors as a houseplant and summers on a porch or patio or poolside. *C. australis*—aka (New Zealand) cabbage palm—is not as easy to own, being capable of maturing into a multitrunk tree form standing 25 or more feet tall. If there is space and a means to overwinter it indoors, it can be grown in a container. Cordylines are members of the Asparagaceae family and cousins to agave. Many cordylines produce flowers followed by berries; container plants outdoors seldom bloom, but houseplants may.

Cordyline is a broadleaf perennial winter-hardy in Zones 9 to 11; plants are treated as annuals or houseplants or overwintered indoors elsewhere.

PLANTING

Cordyline can be propagated from cuttings (aka "Ti logs"): Cut a 3- to 5-inch piece from a leafy head and remove all foliage. (Cut the top of the stem at a slight angle to indicate which end should be up.) Dip the bottom end in rooting hormone. Prepare a mix of sand and peat moss or perlite, dampen it, and insert the stem into it. (See "Pondering Peat Moss," page 22.) A cutting can also be placed in water to a depth of about one-third of its length. Place the cutting in a room with a temperature of at least 60°F where it will receive bright but indirect

RECOMMENDED VARIETIES

- *Cordyline banksii* 'Sprilecpink', aka Electric Pink: hardy in Zones 9 to 11; 4 to 8 feet tall; dark maroon spikes with brilliant pink edges

- *C. fruticosa* 'Exotica': hardy in Zones 10 to 12; 3 to 5 feet tall; variegated green, cream, and pink green leaves

- *C. fruticosa* 'Red Sister': hardy in Zones 9 to 12; up to 6 feet tall; foliage emerges bright pink before gradually darkening to cherry red with burgundy variegation

- *C. fruticosa* 'Singapore Twist': hardy in Zones 9 to 11; up to 8 feet tall; green leaves with burgundy undersides and bright pink stems in fan form

WIT & WISDOM

● *The name "cordyline" comes from the Greek* kordyle,
*meaning "club," which describes the appearance of the plant's root system.
This led to another common name, the club palm.*

● *Do not confuse cordyline with dracaena. The plants may look alike, but they
differ at the root: Cordyline roots are white, while dracaena roots are orange.*

sunlight. Maintain its dampness. Shoots will appear in 4 to 8 weeks (or longer, depending on conditions). Plant when cuttings have four to six leaves.

Cordyline in a container requires a generous base (it develops a taproot), so choose a tall pot whose width is at least 6 inches greater than that of the root ball; go larger if other plants will be grown with the cordyline.

Provide *C. fruticosa* with a rich, well-draining, peaty potting mix (a blend of fine and coarse material, with 30% to 50% organic matter) with a pH of 6.0 to 6.5. *C. australis* is less particular, but potting mix amended with compost is preferable for it.

CARE

For best color, place multicolor cordylines in dappled light; protect them from direct sun, which can burn their leaves. Green-leaf plants do best in direct sun.

Water regularly; cordylines like consistently moist soil but not "wet feet" (standing water) from spring to fall. *C. fruticosa* grown as a houseplant requires watering when the surface of the soil feels dry; provide enough water to cause it to flow out of the container.

Fertilize in spring, if desired, with a granular, slow-release formula or apply a balanced liquid formula at half strength weekly. Avoid fertilizing in winter.

Overwinter cordyline in a bright, sunny spot in a home or greenhouse at 60°F or higher.

Reduce watering in winter.

Provide humidity indoors. Consider placing the plant in a bathroom, setting it on a bed of wet pebbles, and/or misting the foliage.

If the stem becomes leggy and/or foliage unattractive, in late winter remove the foliage top, leaving 1 foot of bare stem. New growth will emerge.

Brown-tip foliage indoors could indicate under- or overwatering, root rot (which can be fatal), excess fertilizer, too-dry air, or fluoride in the water. If the latter is suspected, use bottled and/or distilled water or rainwater.

Yellow foliage could indicate overwatering, too much sunlight, and/or drafts. To address, reduce watering and/or move the plant out of direct sunlight and away from drafts.

DISEASES/PESTS *(see pages 184–200)*

Diseases: bacterial leaf spot, fungal leaf spot, Fusarium root rot. *Pests:* fungus gnats, mealy bugs, scale insects, spider mites, thrips.

ELEPHANT EARS

Colocasia spp., *Alocasia* spp.

I HAVE A MEMORY LIKE AN ELEPHANT.
I REMEMBER EVERY ELEPHANT I EVER MET.
–Herb Caen, American humorist and journalist (1916–97)

Remember this: Few plants rival elephant ears in making a big impression. With their huge, heart-shape leaves in dramatic colors, elephant ears are awesome, elegant, and unforgettable. The common name applies to the subtly different yet equally exotic genera *Colocasia* (kol-oh-KAY-see-ah) and *Alocasia* (ah-loh-KAY-see-ah), each of which has numerous cultivars. Colocasia, the most common of these ornamentals, is a perennial herb also known as taro (whose specific variety is *Colocasia esculenta*). Colocasia

WIT & WISDOM

- *Poi is a Polynesian dish made from mashed up elephant ear corms* (C. esculenta). *It is frequently served at traditional Hawaiian luaus and restaurants.*

- *While most plants known as "elephant ears" are members of the genera* Alocasia *and* Colocasia, *members of other genera in the family Araceae also are sometimes commonly called by the same designation because of their similarly large, arrowhead- or heart-shape leaves. These include but are not limited to* Caladium bicolor, *aka* C. x hortulanum; Philodendron domesticum, *aka* P. hastatum *of gardens;* Xanthosoma lindenii, *aka* C. lindenii, P. lindenii; *and* X. violaceum.

'STINGRAY' ALOCASIA HAS A DISTINCT TAIL AT THE END OF INWARD-CURVING GREEN LEAVES.

will suffer if temperatures fall below 50°F for an extended period. Slightly fragrant flowers may appear under the foliage.

Elephant ears are herbaceous perennials that are winter-hardy in Zones 8 to 12 and overwintered elsewhere.

PLANTING

Propagate by seed or by division. For the latter, divide a colocasia corm in winter or early spring; place in loamy, composted soil in a 1-gallon container; and water consistently.

Plant the corm 4 to 6 inches deep (the bigger the corm, the deeper) in a large container filled with potting mix amended with compost. Set outdoors when temperatures are consistently at least 60°F. If you are adding other plants to the container, consider the exposure that these will need and get, given the size of the elephant ear leaves.

and alocasia grow from corms that are edible when cooked but poisonous when ingested raw. Colocasia leaves form on stems that droop slightly for an umbrella effect; alocasia leaves usually rise up and point upward. Being native to tropical environments, these plants thrive in warm, humid conditions and wet environments (colocasia can be grown in a few inches of standing water) and

CARE

Place in partial or filtered sun, unless noted.

Water regularly and heavily, 2 to 3 inches per week or more, especially for container plants in their preferred weather conditions.

Fertilize with a balanced, slow-release

formula monthly during the growing season.

New leaves will appear throughout the growing season. Use a sharp blade to remove dying ones just above the stem base.

Leaves may be susceptible to high winds. Place plants in a protected area (staking is not generally needed).

Elephant ears are tender perennials; temperatures below 68°F can be injurious. To overwinter, remove the foliage, dig up the corm, set it aside to dry, and pack it in dry wood shavings or peat. (See "Pondering Peat Moss," page 22.) (Break off any small "offsets"—new plants produced by a mother plant complete with their own roots—on the corm; these can be planted in spring as new plants.) Place in a cool, dry area where the temperature does not fall below 45°F. Alternatively, move the plant in its container indoors to a warm, bright location. Remove all but the two top leaves, reduce watering, and cease fertilizing until spring.

DISEASES/PESTS *(see pages 184–200)*
Diseases: bacterial leaf spot, powdery mildew, Pythium root and stem rot, rust, viruses (including dasheen mosaic virus). *Pests:* aphids, scale insects, spider mites, whiteflies.

RECOMMENDED VARIETIES

• *Alocasia* 'Hilo Beauty': irregular cream or yellow flecks on dark green leaves; 2 to 3 feet tall

• *A.* 'Low Rider': compact (dwarf) specimen; heart- or arrowhead-shape, rippled foliage; 1 to 2 feet tall

• *A. macrorrhiza* 'Stingray': distinct tail at the end of inward-curving green leaf; 3 to 6 feet tall

• *Colocasia esculenta* 'Black Magic': first black cultivar; dusty purple-black leaves (with green undertones in shady conditions) on dark petioles; leaves fold upward; reaches 3 to 6 feet tall and wide

• *C. esculenta* 'Coffee Cups': vigorous hybrid; smaller leaves on very tall, dark petioles with leaves folded upward to form cuplike shapes, which collect and release rainwater; spreads 2¹/₂ to 4 feet

• *C. esculenta* 'Illustris', aka Imperial Taro: black-purple leaves patterned with bright green veins; 3 to 5 feet tall

• *C. esculenta* 'Nancy's Revenge': as season progresses, leaves change from all green to having centers of butter yellow at onset of flowering; up to 8 feet tall

• *C. esculenta* 'Pink China': hybrid; green leaves on pinkish stems; one of the hardiest elephant ears, reportedly hardy in Zones 5 and 6 if heavily mulched; up to 6 feet tall

ORNAMENTAL FOUNTAIN GRASS

Pennisetum spp.

IF THE GRASS YOU MOW IS THE ONLY ONE YOU GROW, YOU ARE MISSING OUT!

–Norman Winter, garden writer and lecturer

No mow worries: Ornamental grasses grown in containers are easy to care for and beautiful to behold. Pennisetums are true grasses in the family Poaceae. The genus name derives from the Latin words that describe the seed-head inflorescences: *penna,* meaning feather, and *seta,* for bristle; these features, today commonly referred to as "bottlebrush plumes," are the plants' distinguishing characteristics. As fountain grass sways in a breeze, its elegant plumes dance in the air, adding texture, movement, and interest to a setting. Some 80 *Pennisetum* species offer a wide range of choices from among a group that features single-hue or variegated foliage on stems from 1 to 5 feet tall with 1- to 8-inch-long plumes in several colors. (Specific fountain grass species include *P. alopecuroides, P. glaucum, P. orientale,* and *P. setaceum.*) With so many options, take care to choose the grass that best suits your desire for size, placement, and spread (or lack thereof); these plants can be used as thrillers or fillers with other plants in containers, depending on each plant's needs and growth style, or as singular sensations or solitary accents (see page 97).

Most members of the genus *Pennisetum* are hardy in Zones 5 to 10, depending on variety. Tender varieties are treated as annuals elsewhere.

PLANTING

The propagation of fountain grasses varies. Some self-seed, while others have root balls that can be divided. The seeds of some are sterile, while those of others do not reproduce true to form. Still others are patent-protected and thus restricted. Generally, in cold zones, annual purchases are recommended.

For fountain grass, choose a large container that is at least 8 inches wider than the root ball of the plant.

To eliminate or reduce clogging of the container's drainage holes, line the bottom of the pot with porous landscape fabric or shade cloth.

Provide high-quality potting mix that is well-draining. (Note that the use of ground soil in a container is not recommended.) Soggy or saturated potting mix can cause root rot or disease.

Add some potting mix to the container, then set the plant in it so that the top of the root ball is about 1 inch below the rim. Adjust or add mix accordingly, tamping it down until it is even with the top of the root ball.

Water such that it comes out of the bottom of the container, then add more mix if necessary to regain the level.

Add "spiller" or "filler" plants, if desired. Otherwise or in addition, spread ½ to 1 inch of wood chips or sphagnum moss on the mix to help to conserve moisture.

Place fountain grass where it will receive at least 6 hours of sunlight per day. While these plants can take some shade or dappled light, too much shade will cause the foliage to collapse.

CARE

Water to maintain moisture, but note that once plants are established, they can

---

WIT & WISDOM

- *Large bottlebrush inflorescences make excellent cut flowers alone or in arrangements.*
- *Pennisetum* longistylum *and P.* villosum *are known as "feathertop."*
- *The fountain grass known as "deer grass" (Muhlenbergia rigens) was so named because deer like to lie on beds or mounds of it.*
- *North American indigenous peoples used the stems of deer grass in basketry.*

tolerate some periods of drought.

Fountain grasses have low fertility needs. Apply a balanced, slow-release formula in spring and water-in thoroughly. (Note that too much nitrogen can cause foliage to become floppy.)

Overwintering fountain grasses in cold zones where full-sun greenhouse conditions are not available can be a challenge (*P. setaceum* 'Rubrum' may be an exception). A cool basement with some light may be an option. Bring plants in before the first fall freeze. Provide only enough water to keep roots alive. In spring, remove foliage a few inches above the crown and move the container outdoors, gradually, only after any risk of frost has passed. If the plant does not survive, replace it.

Where grasses are hardy, cut foliage back to 4 to 6 inches above the crown in late winter/early spring before any signs of growth. Failure to do so can delay the warming of the crown and onset of ensuing new growth for up to several weeks.

DISEASES/PESTS *(see pages 184–200)*
Diseases: powdery mildew, rust. *Pests:* aphids, root-knot nematodes, spider mites.

FOUNTAIN GRASSES HAVE LOW FERTILITY NEEDS. APPLY A BALANCED, SLOW-RELEASE FORMULA IN SPRING AND WATER-IN THOROUGHLY.

RECOMMENDED VARIETIES

Dwarf/Miniature (up to approx. 2 feet tall)

• *Pennisetum alopecuroides* 'Burgundy Bunny': hardy in Zones 5 to 9; green foliage has red highlights in summer before turning all-burgundy by fall; cream-color plumes

• *P. alopecuroides* 'Little Bunny': hardy in Zones 5 (with protection) to 9; green foliage; small, buff-color plumes

• *P. alopecuroides* Lumen Gold, aka 'JS Jommenik': hardy in Zones 5 to 8; foliage emerges gold, becomes yellow, then transitions to light green from spring through summer

• *P. alopecuroides* 'Piglet': hardy in Zones 5 to 9; green foliage; pinkish plumes

Semidwarf (approx. 2 to 3 feet tall)

• *P. alopecuroides* 'Cassian': hardy in Zones 5 to 9; grass-green foliage turns orange-red in fall; pale pink plumes

• *P. alopecuroides* 'Hameln': compact; hardy to Zone 5 (in-ground, with protection); bright green foliage; white plumes

• *P. orientale* 'Karley Rose': hardy in Zones 5 to 8; dark green foliage; soft pink plumes

• *P. setaceum* 'Sky Rocket': hardy in Zones 9 to 11; green foliage with white margin; smokey pink plumes that turn cream-color in fall

Medium-Size (approx. 3 to 4 feet tall)

• *P. alopecuroides* 'Red Head': hardy in Zones 5 to 9; dark green foliage; 8-inch-long, reddish-purple plumes

• *P. setaceum* 'Fireworks': hardy in Zones 9 and 10; foliage is variegated, with white and green at the base and cream-color, hot pink, and red in the leaves with burgundy midvein; reddish-purple plumes turn tan in fall; responds favorably to overwintering; propagates by root ball division

• *P. setaceum* 'Rubrum': hardy in Zones 9 and 10; maroon foliage; rosy plumes

Large (up to approx. 5 feet tall)

• *Muhlenbergia rigens*, aka deer grass/meadow muhly: native to Mexico and the southwestern United States; hardy in Zones 6 to 10; gray-green foliage that turns straw-color in fall; purple to yellow plumes on stiff stems ("rigens"); propagates by seed

• *P. alopecuroides* 'Foxtrot': hardy in Zones 5 to 9; green foliage; 4-inch, pale pink plumes

• *P. glaucum* 'Purple Majesty', aka pearl millet: hardy in Zones 2 to 11; deep-purple foliage, stems, and plumes, which are 8 to 14 inches long; propagates from seeds

• *Sporobolus wrightii*, aka giant sacaton: North American native hardy in Zones 5 to 9; green foliage; golden seed heads

SUMMER SNAPDRAGON

Angelonia angustifolia

"I LIKE TO SEE," SAID SHE,
"THE SNAPDRAGON PUT OUT HIS TONGUE TO ME."
–D. H. Lawrence, English writer (1885–1930), in "Snapdragon"

WIT & WISDOM

● Angelonia *'Hilo Princess' debuted in the late 1990s. The Florida Nursery, Growers, and Landscape Association named it a 1998 Plant of the Year. In the seasons since, growers have bred out its loose, leggy form to produce more compact cultivars.*

Snap to it! This performer deserves your attention. Although native to Mexico and the West Indies, summer snapdragon is relatively new to many gardeners. Its heat- and humidity-loving, vigorous spikes grow 12 to 18 inches tall and 12 inches wide and bear two-lipped, slightly scented flowers that evoke its common namesake. The blooms, which are favorites of butterflies and bees, appear in a choice of cheerful colors—blue, mauve, pink, purple, or white—throughout the summer. This is a low-maintenance beauty: Being self-cleaning, it needs no deadheading, and while it likes to drink, it can withstand a drought if it's bedded in organic matter and mulched. The plant is also used in landscape beds and borders.

Summer snapdragon is a tropical perennial that is winter-hardy in Zones 9 to 11. It is treated as an annual elsewhere.

PLANTING
The purchase of seedling plants is recommended. Summer snapdragon can be difficult to overwinter indoors. To start from seeds, sow ⅛ inch deep in moist seed-starting mix 6 to 8 weeks before the last spring frost date. Do not cover seeds with soil, as they need light to germinate. Maintain moisture and keep at 70° to 75°F. Seedlings emerge in 10 to 14 days. At this time, provide sunlight or fluorescent (not incandescent) light for 16 hours per day (plants need a dark period). Minimal fertilizer is needed; feed with a starter solution at half strength during week 3 or 4, if desired. Before planting outdoors, gradually harden off seedlings.

Plant in potting mix that is amended with well-draining organic material (compost and/or aged manure). The medium should retain moisture but not become saturated. Water to keep moist. Mulch to retain moisture.

CARE
Provide 6 to 8 hours of sun per day.

Water when mix feels dry to the touch.

Fertilize monthly with a diluted solution of a 10-5-10 formula (too much may result in more foliage than flowers).

DISEASES/PESTS *(see pages 184–200)*
Disease: powdery mildew. *Pest:* aphids.

RECOMMENDED VARIETIES

● *Angelonia angustifolia* 'Alba': white flowers

● *A. angustifolia* AngelMist Spreading series: large blooms; low-growing; dark-purple, pink, and white flowers

● *A. angustifolia* Serena series: blue, lavender, pink, purple, rose, or white flowers

AFRICAN DAISY

Osteospermum spp.

YOU MAY WEAR YOUR VIRTUES AS A CROWN,
AS YOU WALK THROUGH LIFE SERENELY,
AND GRACE YOUR SIMPLE RUSTIC GOWN
WITH A BEAUTY MORE THAN QUEENLY.
THOUGH ONLY ONE FOR YOU SHALL CARE,
ONE ONLY SPEAK YOUR PRAISES;
AND YOU NEVER WEAR IN YOUR SHINING HAIR,
A RICHER FLOWER THAN DAISIES.

–Phoebe Cary, American poet (1824–71), in "The Fortune in the Daisy"

Daisy-like osteospermums promise good fortune: a wealth of flowers in a kaleidoscope of colors! This South African native, discovered in the 19th century, includes about 70 species of annual, perennial, and shrublike plants. Although "osteos" are in the same Asteraceae family and have flowers that look a lot like those of common daisies, these exotics are dramatically distinguished by brilliant hues and shades. (For years, many people thought that these flowers had been dyed.) Plus, some varieties have spoon-shape petals.

Gardeners loved these features in the original strains but became uninterested as they realized that the flowers closed up at night and on cloudy days. To recapture the public's enthusiasm, breeders set about developing cultivars with blooms that stayed open much longer. Newer varieties have also included other improvements, including increased heat tolerance (the temperature at which buds will develop) and a reduced need for deadheading (now sometimes eliminated).

Today's African daisies are easy to grow, given the proper conditions: full sun, adequate moisture, and moderate temperatures. They are also suitable for growing in-ground.

Also known as Cape daisies and blue-eyed daisies, African daisies are tender herbaceous perennials hardy in Zones 9 to 11 and treated as annuals elsewhere.

PLANTING

Most African daisies are hybrids, so seeds will not produce "true" plants. (Seed-propagated 'Passion Mix' may be an exception to this.) Purchasing new plants or propagating from cuttings is recommended. In autumn, before first frost, prepare a tray or containers with damp, well-draining seed-starter mix. Take 4- to 6-inch cuttings with at least two leaf nodes on each, remove lower leaves and any flower buds, dip the cuttings into rooting hormone, and plant them,

RECOMMENDED VARIETIES

- *Osteospermum* 4D series: uncommon double flowers, with quilled petals in the centers; flowers do not close, bloom all season long; 8 to 12 inches tall

- *O.* 'Astra Purple Spoon': spoonlike petals; blooms from spring through fall; 8 to 18 inches tall

- *O.* 'Bright Lights Red': 8 to 12 inches tall

- *O.* 'Passion Mix': pink, purple, rose, and white flowers; blooms year-round, most profusely in spring; 6 to 18 inches tall

- *O.* Soprano series: many color options; blooms from spring through fall; 8 to 14 inches tall

- *O.* Symphony series: at least five colors—cream-color, lemon, melon, orange, and peach; pinching and deadheading not necessary; 8 to 14 inches tall

WIT & WISDOM

- *Gerbera daisies are sometimes called "African daisies." However, gerberas are generally not as tall and produce larger, more intensely colored flowers.*
- *The genus name* Osteospermum *refers to its hard seeds: In Greek,* osteo *means "bone" and* sperma *means "seed."*

leaving 2 inches of cutting above the soil. Cover with plastic and put them in a mild (60° to 68°F) spot out of direct sunlight. Add bottom heat, if desired. Allow 4 to 6 weeks for rooting, then transplant to potting mix amended with compost and/or aged manure in a well-draining container (at least 4 inches in diameter for a single plant). African daisies like slightly acidic soil (pH of 5.8 to 6.5). Continue growing in a mild environment.

Two weeks before moving African daisies outdoors, gradually harden them off. Purchased seedlings should be planted outdoors after the last frost.

TO PROMOTE BUSHINESSS, PINCH STEMS BEFORE FLOWER BUDS APPEAR.

CARE

African daisies thrive in full sun (partial shade tends to reduce blooms).

Moderate to cool night temperatures (below 55°F) promote flower buds.

Keep the soil evenly moist (about 1 inch per week) but avoid standing water. Soggy soil can encourage root rot.

Apply a balanced fertilizer every 2 to 4 weeks during the growing period.

To promote bushinesss, pinch stems before flower buds appear.

Deadhead to continue blooming unless indicated; some varieties now "bury their dead" (new flowers quickly cover old ones).

As temperatures increase during late spring and early summer, flowering diminishes. Trim plants and continue care, and plants will flower again as temperatures cool in the fall.

Failure to flower can be due to lack of fertilizer (increase frequency); extreme heat or drought (provide plants with shade and/or water); and/or lack of sunlight (increase exposure).

Poor air circulation may promote fungal disease.

African daisies seldom survive a transition indoors, such as to overwinter, without a greenhouse or sunroom.

DISEASES/PESTS *(see pages 184–200)*
Diseases: Phytophthora crown and root rot, powdery mildew, Pythium root and stem rot, Rhizoctonia root and stem rot, Verticillium wilt. *Pests:* aphids, fungus gnats, slugs/snails, spider mites, thrips, whiteflies.

CALADIUM

Caladium bicolor

**GARDENING IS HOW I RELAX. IT'S ANOTHER FORM
OF CREATING AND PLAYING WITH COLOR.**
–Oscar de la Renta, Dominican-born American fashion designer (1932–2014)

Caladiums are nothing if not colorful. The festive foliage of this tropical plant—from its bright midribs to its mottled, veined, and striped leaves in shades of green, white, pink, rose, or red with contrasting margins—adds interest and, when set in motion by a breeze, energy to any setting. And there are thousands from which to choose! Caladiums are members of the arum (Araceae) family. The most cultivated species is *Caladium* x *hortulanum,* aka *C. bicolor,* which is also sometimes called angel wings, heart of Jesus, or mother-in-law plant. Caladiums grow from tubers, which are graded by size: mammoth (3½ inches or larger), jumbo (2½ to 3½ inches), number 1 (1½ to 2½ inches), number 2 (1 to 1½ inches), and number 3, which is even smaller. (Mammoth and jumbo tubers are usually the only ones commercially available.) The larger the tuber, the more leaf buds, but be sure to avoid bruised or soft tubers.

Caladiums bear two main leaf shapes, fancy and lance (or strap). **Fancy-leaf types** produce large, heart-shape leaves supported on petioles that meet the leaves in mid-underside. These caladiums thrive in semishade and may reach 12 to 30 inches in height, depending on cultivar and growing conditions. **Lance- or strap-leaf types** have long, narrow foliage with ruffled edges on petioles that meet them at the center edge of the underside. These usually top out at less than 12 inches tall. Cut leaves can last several days in a vase of fresh flower arrangements.

Caladium is a tropical plant hardy in Zones 9 to 11; it is overwintered or treated as an annual elsewhere.

PLANTING

Before planting, prepare each tuber for optimal foliage production: First, find the largest and/or central bud, which is usually surrounded by several smaller eyes, or buds. You want to remove the largest bud because its presence inhibits the growth of the smaller buds and thus

CALADIUM LEAVES CAN BE MOTTLED, VEINED, OR STRIPED IN SHADES OF GREEN, WHITE, PINK, ROSE, OR RED WITH CONTRASTING MARGINS.

RECOMMENDED VARIETIES

Fancy-Leaf
- *Caladium bicolor* 'Aaron': white leaves with green margins; some sun tolerance
- *C. bicolor* 'Candidum': white leaves with dark green veins
- *C. bicolor* 'Carolyn Whorton': pink leaves with red veins and green margins
- *C. bicolor* 'Fannie Munson': mostly pink leaves with rose-color veins and green margins
- *C. bicolor* 'Red Flash': white-marked green leaves with red veins and wide green margins
- *C. bicolor* 'White Queen': white leaves with red veins and green margins

Lance- or Strap-Leaf
- *C. bicolor* 'Candidum Jr.': white leaves with dark green veins
- *C. bicolor* 'Gingerland': creamy white leaves with red speckles and green margins
- *C. bicolor* 'Miss Muffet': lime green to chartreuse leaves speckled with maroon or deep red
- *C. bicolor* 'Pink Symphony': pink leaves with bright green veins
- *C. bicolor* 'Postman Joyner': red leaves with wide green margins
- *C. bicolor* 'Red Frill': red leaves with dark green margins

more leaves. Using the tip of a sharp knife, cut out the largest bud, being careful not to harm the remaining buds.

Tubers can also be propagated in spring by being cut into pieces that contain at least one bud. Allow pieces to dry for a few days before planting.

Plant tubers outdoors 2 to 3 weeks after the last spring frost date. Set them 2 to 3 inches deep into potting mix with the buds pointing up (smooth side down). Spread 2 to 3 inches of mix on top. In cooler climates, tubers can be sprouted indoors 4 to 6 weeks before planting time. Plant them shallowly in pots or seedling flats. Keep them barely moist and maintain a 70°F environment to encourage growth.

Once tubers are planted, water them frequently and thoroughly. Soil should be evenly moist to the touch but not saturated. Caladium tubers will rot if they are too wet.

CARE

Being tropical plants, caladiums thrive in heat and humidity but usually do not fare well in direct sunlight. For best performance in color and growth, provide dappled or moderate shade and protection from hot afternoon sun. Note that some new cultivars may tolerate a couple of hours of full sun daily; pay attention to specific guidance on plant tags or other descriptions.

Maintain moist soil conditions.

Fertilize every 2 weeks with a balanced liquid formula. Avoid high-phosphorous fertilizers. If fertilizer gets on leaves, they can develop edges that look burned or scorched, aka leaf spot/burn/scorch, a condition that can also be characterized by lower leaves that develop light tan to brown spots and be caused by too much sun or too much water. To prevent/remedy, wash off fertilizer immediately, provide shade, or dry out.

Caladiums rarely but occasionally bloom with a flower that is similar to that of a Jack-in-the-pulpit (*Arisaema tryphyllum*, aka *A. atrorubens*) or calla lily (*Zantedeschia* spp.). However, because the energy used to produce the flower tends to reduce foliage production and the size of the tuber, growers are advised to remove any that appear.

As summer temperatures turn to the cool conditions of fall, caladiums will begin to droop and lose leaves. Lift tubers (with some foliage attached, which will help to identify the variety) or bring containers indoors when nighttime temperatures drop below 60°F. Tubers can be saved to regrow in the following year; note, however, that white-foliage tubers tend to overwinter best and that foliage on second-year plants may not be as abundant as it was during the first year. (For this reason, combining old and new tubers in a planting is recommended.)

To save tubers, spread them out to dry in a place that is safe from cold, rain, and direct sun. Allow 2 to 3 weeks, or until the foliage is tan and papery. Gather together like varieties and remove their foliage. Discard any that are diseased or soft. Pack by types in mesh bags or loosely in dry peat moss, perlite, or vermiculite. (See "Pondering Peat Moss," page 22.) Store in a dry area with a temperature of at least 60°F. Avoid refrigeration and high humidity. Prepare as directed to replant in spring.

DISEASES/PESTS *(see pages 184–200)*
Diseases: Fusarium tuber rot, southern blight. *Pests:* aphids, mealy bugs, root-knot nematodes, spider mites, thrips, whiteflies.

WIT & WISDOM

• *Caladium tubers are poisonous if eaten.*

• *While most plants known as "elephant ears" are members of the genera* Alocasia *and* Colocasia, *members of other genera in the family Araceae also are sometimes commonly called by the same designation because of their similarly large, arrowhead- or heart-shape leaves. These include but are not limited to* Caladium bicolor, *aka* C. x hortulanum; Philodendron domesticum, *aka* P. hastatum *of gardens;* Xanthosoma lindenii, *aka* C. lindenii, P. lindenii; *and* X. violaceum.

• *Discovered in the Amazon River basin, caladiums have been cultivated in Europe since the late 1700s.*

COLEUS

Solenostemon scutellarioides varieties, aka *Plectranthus scutellarioides*

**GRAMMATICALLY, IF YOU WERE WRITING A TREATISE ON LATIN,
OR CONVERSING IN THE LATIN TONGUE, YOU WOULD MAKE
COLEUS FOR THE SINGULAR AND COLEI FOR THE PLURAL.
BUT COLEUS HAS BEEN MADE A PART OF THE ENGLISH LANGUAGE
BY ITS EVERYDAY USE. . . . IT WILL THEREFORE BE QUITE
SAFE, WHEN TALKING TO YOUR NEIGHBOR, TO SAY "COLEUS"
FOR THE SINGULAR AND "COLEUSES" FOR THE PLURAL.**

–Thomas Meehan, English-born nurseryman and writer (1826–1901), in
The Gardener's Monthly and Horticulturist, *Vol. 21 (1879)*

With hundreds of varieties displaying many different vibrant shades of numerous colors (e.g., nearly black, bronze, burgundy, cream-color, green, orange, pink, red, yellow, and white) in dramatic ways (e.g., borders, dots, splashes, splotches, streaks, and veins) on large to small leaves with wild shapes and styles (e.g., crinkled, elongated, fingerlike, lobed, ruffled, scalloped, twisted, and webbed), coleuses always liven up drab spaces. The fodder for fascination flows not only from their forms, though: Consider cultivar names such as 'Alabama Sunset', 'Buttercream', 'Campfire', 'Carnival', 'Dark Heart', 'Dragon's Claw', 'Duke of Swirl', 'Florida Sunshine', and 'Solar Eclipse'—to name but a few.

Although coleuses have square stems like other members of the mint family (Lamiaceae), they display none of their cousins' invasive qualities. Native to Africa, India, Sri Lanka, and Southeast Asia, coleuses take three plant forms— **upright, rounded,** and **trailing**—and range in height from 6 to 36 inches.

Also known as flame nettle, painted nettle, and painted leaf, coleus is a winter-hardy herbaceous perennial in Zones 10 and 11 that is treated as an annual elsewhere.

RECOMMENDED VARIETIES

Sun-Tolerant

• *Solenostemon scutellarioides* 'Alabama Sunset': chartreuse, orange, and red colors intensify in sunlight; upright form; 12 to 24 inches tall

• *S. scutellarioides* 'Burgundy Wedding Train': heart-shape burgundy leaves outlined in lime green; trailing habit; 12 to 18 inches tall

• *S. scutellarioides* 'Pineapple': lime-green foliage outlined in burgundy; upright form; 12 to 18 inches tall

• *S. scutellarioides* 'Redhead': bright red foliage; rounded form; 18 to 24 inches tall

Partial Shade

• *S. scutellarioides* 'Black Magic': velvety, dark purple foliage with chartreuse scalloped edges; rounded form; 18 to 24 inches tall

• *S. scutellarioides* 'Dark Star': deep purple foliage; upright form; 24 inches tall

• *S. scutellarioides* 'Fishnet Stockings': green leaves with dark purple veining; upright form; 12 to 36 inches tall

• *S. scutellarioides* 'Freckles': bronze and orange splashes on pale yellow leaves; upright form; 12 to 24 inches tall

• *S. scutellarioides* 'India Frills': lime-green foliage with splashes of orange, pink, and purple; compact, trailing form; 6 to 12 inches tall

PLANTING

Purchasing new plants or starting coleuses from cuttings is recommended. Take 4- to 6-inch cuttings in fall before the first frost. Cut right above a leaf node, then remove lower leaves. Place in a glass jar filled with water. When roots are 1 to 2 inches long, transplant to a small pot filled with potting mix. Grow these in a sunny window or under lights. Maintain moisture and mist to aid humidity.

Plants can also be started from seeds (note that seeds do not produce identical plants; use cuttings, if this is the goal); set seeds on the surface of 3 inches of seed-starting mix 8 to 10 weeks before the last frost date. Supply with light (for germination) and transplant outdoors when evening temperatures are consistently at least 60°F.

COLEUSES WERE ONCE CONSIDERED SHADE OR DAPPLED-SUNLIGHT PLANTS.

Provide potting mix amended with compost.

Coleuses thrive in heat up to 95°F; plants will languish in temperatures below 55°F, and leaves will fall off in colder conditions.

Avoid windy locations; extreme winds can cause stems to break.

Water thoroughly after planting and keep roots consistently moist for the first 7 to 10 days. Good drainage is essential; "wet feet" (excessive water) can result in stunted growth and brown foliage.

CARE

Provide proper light exposure for the variety. Although coleuses were once considered shade or dappled-sunlight plants only, breeders have now developed full sun–tolerant varieties.

COLEUSES DISPLAY NO INVASIVE QUALITIES.

WIT & WISDOM

● *British and American Victorians used coleuses in elaborate*
"carpet gardens" and "carpet bedding," which were living mosaics
of outdoor plants that often mirrored indoor rug patterns.

● *Research has shown that within several hours after a coleus stem*
is wounded, some of its cells around the wound immediately start to divide.
After 2 days or so, some of these cells differentiate into a
different cell type that can transport water around the wound.

Generally, dark-leaf varieties are more sun-tolerant, while plants with lighter foliage need more shade. For all, avoid deep shade.

Water when the soil is dry at a 1 inch depth. Water the soil and base of the plant; avoid wetting the foliage.

Slow-release balanced formula fertilizers are suggested at half strength every 2 weeks. Excess fertilizer can weaken the leaf colorization.

Pinch back flower spikes to maintain bushiness and plant vigor. (Trailing varieties are the most likely to bloom.) Note that the tiny flowers are not without appeal: They appear in shades of blue, purple, and white on spikes that lure hummingbirds. Spikes gathered in a bouquet can be attractive. Many new cultivars have been bred to be slow bloomers, almost eliminating the need for them to be pinched back.

Even under the best conditions (70°F environment and adequate light, indoors or in a greenhouse), coleuses that are overwintered indoors are vulnerable to diseases, pests, or blooming, which tends to reduce vigor and hasten the plant's decline.

COMBINE A VARIETY OF COLEUSES TO ADD MORE INTEREST TO A CONTAINER.

DISEASES/PESTS *(see pages 184–200)*
Diseases: Botrytis blight, downy mildew, Pythium root and stem rot, Rhizoctonia root and stem rot. *Pests:* aphids, mealy bugs, slugs/snails, spider mites, whiteflies.

MOSS ROSE

Portulaca grandiflora

THE TWILIGHT FALLS ON THE GARDEN, /
MOTHER'S GARDEN. / IN FANCY, I HEAR THE SWISH OF HER DRESS /
AS SHE GATHERS FORGET-ME-NOTS. /
AND THE MOSS ROSE WHISPERS / TO THE WIND.
–Newfoundland Quarterly, *Vol. 20 (1920–21)*

Moss rose is easy to love. Native to the arid plains of Argentina, southern Brazil, and Uruguay, this semi-succulent in the purslane family (Portulacaceae) thrives in Zones 2 to 11 in this hemisphere. Its single, semidouble, and double rose-like flowers, in a wide range of hues that include white as well as cheerful pastels—fuchsia, lavender, magenta, orange, peach, pink, purple, and yellow—rise above its bright green, needle-like leaves to inspire a festive mood when draping from hanging baskets or filling containers. This low grower typically spreads a foot or more, while its blooms, ranging from 1 to 3 inches in diameter, rise up over the foliage.

Portulaca grandiflora demands little in terms of care but spreads joy and delight wherever it grows—as long as the Sun shines. Flowers on some plants close on cloudy or rainy days and from sundown to sun-up; newer cultivars may hold their blooms longer.

Moss rose, aka Sun plant or Sun rose, is considered an herbaceous perennial in Zones 9 to 11 and treated as a tender annual elsewhere.

PLANTING

Purchasing seedlings or starter plants may jump-start moss rose's flowering period, but it can also be grown from seeds or propagated through cuttings from established plants. Start seeds in seed-starting mix indoors 6 to 8 weeks before the last frost. Cover minimally; moss rose needs sunlight to germinate. Dampen and maintain moisture. Plants germinate in about 10 to 14 days in 70° to 85°F temperatures. To propagate from a cutting, prepare damp potting mix. Trim off a 3-inch piece of the plant and remove any foliage from the last inch of the cut end. Insert the cut end into the potting mix. Maintain even moisture until new growth appears,

RECOMMENDED VARIETIES

- *Portulaca grandiflora* 'Afternoon Delight': 2-inch flowers in numerous hues stay open longer than those of other varieties

- *P. grandiflora* 'Calypso Mix': not as fast-growing as others; requires consistently moist soil; orange, pink, red, and yellow flowers

- *P. grandiflora* Happy Hour series: bred to bloom earlier in season; large, double blooms in vivid colors attract butterflies and hummingbirds

- *P. grandiflora* Sundance series: semidouble flowers in a multitude of colors remain open most of the day

- *P. grandiflora* Sundial series: early-flowering variety; double flowers in numerous colors open in cooler and cloudy weather

WIT & WISDOM

- *Portulaca oleracea, common purslane with flat, fleshy leaves that is sometimes grown as a vegetable and often considered a weed, is known as "moss rose."*
- *Portulacas have been grown in American gardens since the 1700s.*
- *"Portulaca" comes from the Latin words* porto, *meaning "to carry," and* lac *meaning "milk," referring to the milky sap of some species.*

PURCHASING SEEDLINGS OR STARTER PLANTS MAY JUMP-START MOSS ROSE'S FLOWERING PERIOD.

then transplant.

Be aware that moss rose transplants need special care: The night before transplanting, water to ensure that the plant is hydrated so that soil will cling to its shallow roots. Lift with a spoon or small spade (depending on plant size), including the soil surrounding the plant. Space plants 6 to 12 inches apart; crowded plants flower poorly. Replant, with roots only just below the soil's surface, as soon as possible. Water lightly and keep moist until new growth appears (this is a sign that the plant is established). Moss rose's shallow root system means that water is important until plants get going. Afterward, too much water can cause rot, which is why well-draining soil is essential.

CARE

Moss rose is drought-tolerant but benefits from watering when the top inch of soil is dry.

Provide 6 to 8 or more hours of sunlight per day; warm temperatures are ideal. Shade may reduce blooms.

Deadhead to stimulate more blooms or to deter self-seeding, if desired.

If plants become leggy, pinch stems back and provide a diluted dose of balanced fertilizer. New growth and blooms should follow.

DISEASES/PESTS *(see pages 184–200)*

Diseases: none serious; sometimes Botrytis blight, damping off, Pythium root and stem rot, Rhizoctonia root and stem rot. *Pests:* aphids, slugs/snails.

PELARGONIUM/GERANIUM

Pelargonium spp.

SCIENCE, OR PARASCIENCE, TELLS US THAT GERANIUMS BLOOM BETTER IF THEY ARE SPOKEN TO. BUT A KIND WORD EVERY NOW AND THEN IS REALLY QUITE ENOUGH. TOO MUCH ATTENTION, LIKE TOO MUCH FEEDING, AND WEEDING AND HOEING, INHIBITS AND EMBARRASSES THEM.
–Victoria Glendinning, English writer and broadcaster (b. 1937)

WIT & WISDOM

● *"Pelargonium" derives from the ancient Greek word*
pelargos *for stork, while "Geranium" comes from the Greek word* geranos,
for crane; the fruit of both resemble a bird's beak.

● *As companion plants to cabbages, corn, peppers, roses, and tomatoes,
pelargoniums repel cabbageworms and Japanese beetles.*

At once old-fashioned and yet always in fashion, pelargoniums, commonly called geraniums, are among the easiest plants to care for despite being perhaps the most confusingly named. We are speaking here of annual pelargoniums, rather than true geraniums, or cranesbills. The nomenclature around these beauties originates with ever-curious plant-hunting botanists. In 1753, Sweden's Carl Linnaeus identified the genus *Geranium,* embracing all species. Some three decades later, French enthusiast Charles Louis L'Héritier de Brutelle created the *Pelargonium* genus for the semi-tender to tender annual plants native mostly to South Africa, at the same time leaving the herbaceous perennial types (cranesbills), in the *Geranium* genus. Then, in the 1820s, *Geraniaceae,* a five-volume collection by English botanist Robert Sweet, attempted to define a single family by the same name that is used for classification today. These days, growers and enthusiasts endeavor to maintain the difference because, in fact, the plants are not so similar.

Pelargonium includes about 200 species, with the most common being the tender annuals known for their long stems usually topped by pink, purple, red, salmon, or white flower umbels (clusters) that appear from spring until frost. Pelargoniums can be overwintered for the following year.

True geraniums are herbaceous perennials that feature less showy flowers and enjoy bloom periods from spring into early fall.

PLANTING

Purchasing pelargoniums or propagating them from stem cuttings taken from late summer to early fall is recommended. Cut a 3- to 4-inch stem and remove lower leaves. Dip the cut end in rooting hormone and plant in potting mix.

Pelargoniums can also be grown from seeds set indoors. Flowering occurs in 3 to 4 months.

Once roots are established, plant seedlings or cuttings in a container filled with potting mix amended with organic matter (compost and/or aged manure). Add a slow-release fertilizer at the time of planting.

The soil must be well-draining, lest stem and root rot result.

Move outdoors after all danger of frost has passed.

CARE

Pelargoniums enjoy full sun; plants may benefit from light shade in the heat of the day.

Water regularly, allowing the soil to dry out between waterings (dry spells can be tolerated). Avoid soggy soil.

Fertilize containers every 2 to 4 weeks with a slow-release balanced formula or half-strength liquid solution. Do not overfertilize, which can inhibit blooms.

Deadhead to prolong flowering, and pinch stems to encourage bushiness.

To overwinter as houseplants, bring containers indoors before the first frost.

Provide with a sunny spot (a southern or western exposure is ideal) in a cool area (60° to 65°F during the day and slightly cooler at night); avoid extreme temperatures or drafts. Reduce watering.

Alternatively, lift (dig up) plants and shake soil off the roots. Store one or two plants in a large paper sack or hang the plants upside down in a cool, dry location.

Check plants periodically. If they seem too dry, soak their roots in water for a few hours, dry, and then return to the bag or hanging position. In March, cut back the stems to green tissue and trim

RECOMMENDED VARIETIES

Pelargonium Types

• Interspecific: zonal and ivy hybrids; nonstop flower producers

• Ivy (*Pelargonium peltatum*): named for a trailing habit and ivy-like foliage; single, semidouble, or double flowers; colors include bicolor, burgundy, pink, purple, red, salmon, and white

• Regal, aka 'Martha Washington' (*P. x domesticum*): bicolor burgundy, lavender, pink, and white blooms; fussy—prefers cool, wet, climate conditions to hot, humid, and/or sunny; inappropriate conditions will reduce flower production; often a houseplant

• Scented: foliage yields scent (cedar, lemon, lime, mint, orange, and rose) when brushed or rubbed; note that 'Citronella' does not repel mosquitoes; pink or white flowers are smaller than those of zonals

• Seed: similar to zonals; propagated by seeds; slower-growing, shorter, more compact than zonals; smaller but more numerous flowers than zonals; flowers "shatter" (are shed naturally)

• Variegated: a form of zonal; bi- or tricolor foliage; tends to have fewer flowers than other zonal types

• Zonal (*P. x hortorum*): the most common form; "zonal" refers to patterns on the leaves that darken with maturity; propagated by cuttings; single or double flowers; colors include bicolor, orange, purple, red, salmon, and white

TO OVERWINTER PELARGONIUMS AS HOUSEPLANTS, BRING CONTAINERS INDOORS BEFORE THE FIRST FROST AND PROVIDE WITH A SUNNY SPOT (A SOUTHERN OR WESTERN EXPOSURE IS IDEAL).

the roots to remove dead material. Soak the roots and then plant in container(s), water thoroughly, and place in a sunny location. Move outdoors when all danger of frost has passed.

To overwinter pelargoniums as dormant plants, bring their containers into a cool, dark area of the basement or a frost-free garage before the first frost. Allow the soil to dry out. Check periodically, and if signs of drying are present, water slightly. To bring out of dormancy, cut back the stems to live tissue, water thoroughly, and place in a sunny location before moving outdoors once the threat of frost has passed. Dormancy will promote vigorous flowering in the next growing season.

DISEASES/PESTS *(see pages 184–200)*
Diseases: bacterial leaf spot, Botrytis blight, Pythium root and stem rot (aka "blackleg"), rust, southern bacterial wilt, viruses. *Pests:* aphids, cabbage loopers, spider mites, tobacco budworms, whiteflies.

WISHBONE FLOWER

Torenia fournieri

**TO SUCCEED IN LIFE, YOU NEED THREE THINGS: A WISHBONE,
A BACKBONE, AND A FUNNY BONE.**

–Reba McEntire, American singer, songwriter, and actress (b. 1955)

WIT & WISDOM

• *The tradition of treasuring the furcula ("little fork" in Latin)—the forked bone found at the front of most birds' breasts—dates from the Etruscans, an ancient Italian civilization. They believed poultry to be oracles and this bone the key to a bird's prescience. After a bird died, they would dry the bone in the sun; later it could be picked up and rubbed by those who passed by in order to get wishes granted—hence, "wishbone."*

No bones about it: This plant makes wishes come true. Look closely at the trumpet-shape flowers for the plant's eponymous feature: A pair of stamens unite at the anthers in a way that resembles a wishbone, a part found in chickens, turkeys, and other birds. Wishbone flower grows well in shade or semi-shade (even indoors), if adequate moisture is maintained; legginess is a clue that more light is needed. Note that most cultivars are intolerant of sun and high heat. (The greater the amount of light that a wishbone flower can receive and tolerate, the wider the choices available as companion plants in containers; growth habits should be compatible.) Wishbone flower's color appears not only in its blooms— its foliage can turn red or bronze in unseasonably cold weather.

Also known as bluewings, *Torenia fournieri* is a perennial grown as an annual.

PLANTING

Purchasing wishbone flower or starting its seeds indoors 8 to 12 weeks before the last spring frost in a 70° to 75°F environment are options. For the latter, do not cover: Light aids germination, which can take 7 to 15 days.

Plant 1 to 2 weeks after the last spring frost date.

Provide a well-draining medium; use potting mix amended with organic matter (compost and/or aged manure).

CARE

Place wishbone flower where it will be in partial to full shade.

Water for consistent moisture, not saturation.

Apply a balanced fertilizer every 2 weeks during the growing season.

Deadheading is not necessary; plants are self-cleaning.

Failure to bloom usually indicates too much shade and a need for sunlight.

If trailing, avoid pinching, as this promotes bushy growth.

DISEASES/PESTS *(see pages 184–200)*
Diseases: powdery mildew, Pythium root and stem rot, viruses. *Pests:* aphids, whiteflies.

RECOMMENDED VARIETIES

• *Torenia fournieri* Moon series: purple and yellow shades

• *T. fournieri* Panda series: wide range of colorful flower hues; compact, at 4 to 8 inches tall

• *T. fournieri* Summer Wave series: tolerant of heat and drought; blue, rose, silver, and violet shades

BACOPA

Chaenostoma cordatum, aka *Sutera cordata*

**I WISH ONE COULD PRESS
SNOWFLAKES IN A BOOK LIKE FLOWERS.**
–James Schuyler, American poet (1923–91)

Let it snow! The *Chaenostoma cordatum,* aka *Sutera cordata,* cultivar 'Snowflake' offers a blizzard of crisp, white, five-lobe flowers and evergreen foliage on lush, trailing stems. A South African native, what we know today as *C. cordatum* has been the subject of a number of genus reassignments and common name changes since the early part of the 19th

WIT & WISDOM

● *The* Bacopa *genus, commonly known as water hyssop, includes more than 70 aquatic plants that are typically found growing in moist areas such as marshes, bogs, and water gardens and along streams and rivers. Its members have white flowers and small, relatively thick, succulent evergreen leaves.*

century and been known at one time or another as *Sutera diffusus, Bacopa cordata* (which is technically incorrect, inasmuch as *Bacopa* is the genus for water hyssop), and simply "bacopa."

This fast-growing plant blooms abundantly from late spring to first fall frost in sun, with adequate water. Although best known for its white flowers, bacopa also has cultivars that produce flowers in blue, pink, and purple. Bacopa is also grown as a ground cover.

C. cordatum is a winter annual or perennial in Zones 9 to 11 and treated as an annual elsewhere.

PLANTING

Bacopa can be propagated by cuttings, but gardeners are advised to purchase plants.

The plant is not particular about pH or soil, but its medium must drain well. It can not tolerate standing water, which may lead to root rot. Plant in a container or hanging basket in potting mix amended with compost or organic matter.

CARE

Provide bacopa with full sun to partial shade, with consistent moisture, or give it morning sun and afternoon shade. Note that extreme heat may cause it to lose vigor.

Water generously and regularly; avoid complete dryness. Bloom and bud drop may be a sign of drought stress. If this occurs and is not severe, continue watering and allow about 2 weeks for blooms to return.

Apply a balanced liquid fertilizer (10-10-10) every 1 to 2 weeks.

Bacopa is self-cleaning; no deadheading is necessary.

Prune to remove dead stems under foliage, if necessary.

DISEASES/PESTS *(see pages 184–200)*
Diseases: Botrytis blight, Phytophthora crown and root rot, powdery mildew, viruses. *Pests:* aphids, thrips, whiteflies.

RECOMMENDED VARIETIES

● *Chaenostoma cordatum* 'Blue Showers': lavender-blue flowers

● *C. cordatum* MegaCopa series 'Pink Shine': large pink flowers

● *C. cordatum* Snowstorm series 'Giant Snowflake': large (12-inch), white flowers; vigorous grower

● *C. cordatum* Snowstorm series 'Snow Globe': large white flowers

FAIRY FAN-FLOWER

Scaevola aemula

THE FANS MAKE THE PERSON A STAR.
–Zac Efron, American actor (b. 1987)

WIT & WISDOM

● *Based on* scaevus, *Latin for "left-handed," the word* Scaevola *was once given as a surname to the family of Roman soldier Gaius Mucius (c. 509 B.C.), who deliberately burned his right hand to demonstrate courage to enemy captors. Its use as the genus name for fairy fan-flower stems from the hand-like nature of the plant's blooms.*

Fan out! This Australian native plant, named for the fan-like shape of its half-circle, five-petal (or -finger) flowers with yellow "throats," thrives on heat. Blooms in several colors—blue, pink, purple, or white—and sizes appear profusely throughout summer to first frost. Depending on the cultivar, trailing stems can reach 2 or more feet long. The flowers attract butterflies, bees, and other pollinators. It is also used as a ground cover.

Also known simply as "fan-flower," scaevola is treated as a tender perennial in Zones 10 and 11 and as an annual elsewhere.

PLANTING
Purchasing plants or starting seeds indoors 6 to 8 weeks before the last frost date are both options. The most common growing method is by propagating 4- to 6-inch-long flower-

RECOMMENDED VARIETIES

● *Scaevola aemula* 'Blue Wonder': one of the first developed; violet-blue flowers

● *S. aemula* Bombay series: blue, pink, or white flowers

● *S. aemula* Whirlwind series: blue, pink, or white flowers

free vegetative cuttings. Remove leaves from the bottom half of the cutting and dip the cut end in rooting hormone. Plant in slightly moist, well-draining, and warm (70° to 75°F) potting mix.

Avoid overwatering, which can slow rooting or possibly cause rot. Bottom heat may hasten rooting. To improve overall performance later, pinch cuttings once the roots are set. Those rooted in containers in autumn and maintained in a bright, cool, indoor environment can be moved outdoors in spring once the threat of frost has passed.

CARE
Place in full sun to partial shade or filtered/dappled sunlight. Water regularly to keep the soil evenly moist but not wet.

To prevent root rot, allow the soil to dry out slightly between waterings.

Fertilize regularly with a low-phosphorus product to promote flowering. The plant is sensitive to phosphorus, which can cause foliage discoloration and/or desiccation.

Fan-flower is self-cleaning; deadheading is not necessary. Container plants may be overwintered indoors.

DISEASES/PESTS *(see pages 184–200)*
Diseases: none serious; sometimes black root rot, Botrytis blight, Pythium root and stem rot. *Pests:* none serious; sometimes aphids, mealy bugs, scale insects, thrips.

LICORICE PLANT

Helichrysum petiolare

WE'RE LIKE LICORICE. NOT EVERYBODY LIKES LICORICE, BUT THE PEOPLE WHO LIKE LICORICE REALLY LIKE LICORICE.
–Jerry Garcia, American musician (1942–95)

Taste is a matter of style (not palate) when considering this plant, as it is inedible. Licorice plant's common name comes from the faint scent emitted by its velvety leaves on trailing stems, especially in the heat of summer. In its second year, this plant may produce tiny white flowers; these are considered insignificant and are often removed as they appear in order to direct energy to the leaves. This plant has a mounding form and a spread of up to 3 feet.

Licorice plant is a woody, tender, evergreen perennial, winter-hardy in Zones 9 to 11 and treated as an annual elsewhere.

PLANTING

Although licorice plant seeds may be available (note that cultivars may not come true from seeds), purchasing specific cultivars as seedlings or propagating vegetatively from cuttings from an existing plant is recommended. Cut a 4- to 6-inch-long stem right above a leaf node, then remove lower leaves. Dip the stem and up to two leaves in rooting hormone. Plant, covering the leaves with rooting hormone, in a container filled with potting mix and coarse sand. Water regularly and provide bright, indirect light. Roots should develop after 3 to 4 weeks.

Plant outside after last spring frost date.

RECOMMENDED VARIETIES

• *Helichrysum petiolare* 'Lemon Licorice': leaves emerge silver, then turn yellow-green

• *H. petiolare* 'Licorice Splash': variegated gray-green and creamy white leaves

• *H. petiolare* 'Limelight': lime green leaves

• *H. petiolare* 'White Licorice': silver-white, frosted-looking leaves

Licorice plant is quite tolerant of soil conditions but benefits from amendments. It will grow in most soils, including poor; a container filled with potting mix amended with organic material or compost is ideal.

It is drought-tolerant once established but prefers regular watering.

CARE

Grow in full sun to partial shade. Shade tends to reduce vigor but can provide relief and help to maintain the plant's visual appeal in extreme heat.

Provide even moisture in the U.S. South and West; elsewhere, water when the top 1 to 2 inches of soil are dry. Avoid standing water or saturated soil to mitigate the risk of root rot.

Apply a balanced fertilizer in midseason.

Pinch back stems to have a fuller (or smaller) plant.

As older stems turn brown, cut them off to improve the plant's appearance.

To overwinter, cut stems back hard and place the plant in a sunny window.

DISEASES/PESTS *(see pages 184–200)*

Diseases: Botrytis blight, Pythium root and stem rot. *Pests:* none serious; sometimes aphids, leaf miners, whiteflies.

WIT & WISDOM

• *The name* Helichrysum *comes from the Greek words* helios, *meaning "Sun," and* chrysos, *meaning "golden."*

• *The word "licorice" derives from an ancient Greek word that translates as "sweet root."*

• *Do not confuse with* Glycyrrhiza glabra, *a perennial legume whose woody root is boiled for use in food and medicines.*

NASTURTIUM

Tropaeolum majus

**NASTURTIUMS, WHO COLORED YOU,
YOU WONDERFUL, GLOWING THINGS? YOU MUST HAVE
BEEN FASHIONED OUT OF SUMMER SUNSETS.**
–Lucy Maud Montgomery, Canadian writer (1874–1942), in Emily Climbs

Nasturtiums inspire glowing reviews wherever they appear. This easy-to-grow plant bears abundant blooms up to 2½ inches wide from spring to fall in shades of cream, orange, pink, red, white, and yellow in jewel tones and muted pastels on vines from 3 to 10 feet long. For containers, choose the trailing or climbing types (*Tropaeolum majus*, aka Indian cress or "common"/"garden" nasturtium) or risk being disappointed, as dwarf, aka bush, varieties *(T. minus)* form bunched mounds. All parts of nasturtiums except the roots are edible. The flowers have a spicy fragrance and peppery taste that intensifies in hot weather. The leaves have a more potent peppery flavor, while the stems have a bit more bite. Seedpods may be pickled and used like capers.

Nasturtium is winter-hardy in Zones 9 to 11 and treated as a warm-weather annual elsewhere.

PLANTING

For best results, scarify (nick or scratch with a fingernail file or sandpaper) to reveal a bit of the pale interior. Alternatively, soak seeds overnight or until they are slightly swollen. Sow immediately at a depth of ½ inch.

Outdoors, direct-seed them into a container filled with potting mix after the threat of frost has passed. Indoors, start them 2 to 4 weeks before the last frost. Be aware that the plant's fragile roots are sensitive to transplanting.

CARE

Nasturtium grows best in full sun; plants will tolerate partial shade but will not bloom as well.

Water regularly but not to excess. Nasturtium tolerates some drought but performs best in moist, well-draining soil. Note that water-stressed plants have subpar blooms and flavor.

Heat stress can also halt blooming.

Trim back periodically to prevent the crowding out of other plants and to encourage more foliage.

Avoid fertilizer, especially nitrogen:

It tends to increase foliage and decrease flower output. Deadhead (cut off) spent flowers to promote more blooms.

DISEASES/PESTS (see pages 184–200)

Diseases: bacterial leaf spot, southern bacterial wilt, viruses. *Pests:* aphids, cabbage loopers, corn earworms (aka tomato fruitworms), flea beetles, imported cabbageworms, leaf miners, slugs/snails, whiteflies.

RECOMMENDED VARIETIES

- *Tropaeolum majus* 'Alaska Mix': variegated foliage; flowers in an array of colors

- *T. majus* 'Amazon Jewel': variegated foliage; gemstone flowers of gold, pale lemon, orange, peachy-rose, and ruby

- *T. majus* 'Empress of India': heirloom; blue-green foliage; scarlet flowers

- *T. majus* 'Jewel of Africa': variegated foliage; cream-color, orange, peachy-pink, scarlet, and yellow flowers

- *T. majus* 'Moonlight': green foliage; pale yellow flowers

WIT & WISDOM

- *Every spring, as many as 10 gardeners at the Isabella Stewart Gardner Museum in Boston, Massachusetts, hang baskets of nasturtiums on the balconies above its courtyard, from which fall 20-foot-long trailing vines. Seeds for the plants are started in June and then trained at the museum's greenhouses throughout the winter to be ready for the following spring's exhibition. The display lasts about 3 weeks.*

SILVER NICKEL VINE

Dichondra argentea 'Silver Falls'

SILVER, GOLD—I DON'T DISCRIMINATE. I LOVE SPARKLY THINGS.
–Charlaine Harris, American writer (b. 1951)

WIT & WISDOM

- Dichondra argentea *is part of the Convolvulaceae family, whose members are commonly known as bindweeds or morning glories.*
- *Do not confuse with* D. carolinensis, *aka Carolina ponysfoot (a green creeping herb), or* D. repens, *aka kidney weed (a deep-green ground cover).*

All that glitters is not gold: *Dichondra argentea* 'Silver Falls,' aka silver nickel vine, produces a cascade of kidney-shape silvery foliage. Its pewtery metallic appearance is a cool contrast to deep green foliage and the primary hues of companion plants. Very small greenish-yellow or white flowers may appear from May to June but are considered insignificant.

Described as the "Niagara Falls of trailers" for its fast-growing habit and trailing stems up to 5 feet long, this super spiller has high tolerance for heat and drought, making it ideal for low-water or xeriscape environments.

Silver nickel vine is a tender herbaceous perennial native to West Texas and Mexico. It is winter-hardy in Zones 9 to 11 and treated as an annual elsewhere.

PLANTING

Purchasing plants is recommended; silver nickel vine seeds are available mainly only to wholesalers.

Plant silver nickel vine in potting mix amended with sandy loam. Fertilize with a slow-release balanced formula.

CARE

Provide the plant with full sun; it does tolerate some light shade.

Silver nickel vine prefers dry to medium-moist conditions; overwatering or standing water puts it at risk of dying. Less than an inch of water per week is advised, except in extreme heat, when more can be given. If the plant wilts, all is not lost; it should recover with watering.

No pinching or pruning is needed.

No fertilizer is necessary after initial planting.

DISEASES/PESTS *(see pages 184–200)*
Diseases: none serious. *Pest:* flea beetles.

RECOMMENDED VARIETIES
This is a singular species.

'SILVER FALLS' PLANTED WITH ALYSSUM AND TWO VARIETIES OF CORAL BELLS

SWEET POTATO VINE

Ipomoea batatas

MINE IS THE TIME OF FOLIAGE,
WHEN HILLS AND VALLEYS TEEM
WITH BUDS AND VINES SWEET-SCENTED,
ALL CLOTHED IN GLOWING GREEN.
–*Mary Weston Fordham, American poet and teacher (c. 1843–1905)*

WIT & WISDOM

• *The sweet potato is a symbol of good luck in many cultures.*

• *The genus name is thought to come from the Greek words* ips, *for "worm," and* homoios, *for "resembling"—referencing the way in which the plant spreads roots underground. The word* batatas *means "potato" in the indigenous Caribbean Taíno culture.*

• *Do not confuse with wild potato vine* (Ipomoea pandurata).

Container gardeners everywhere have a sweet spot for sweet potato vines. Their lush, leafy, vividly colored trailing vines (falling as much as 10 feet) add contrast, cover, and "kick" to container arrangements. Ornamental cultivars have been bred for visual appeal, not growers' appetites. These sweets are eye candy: Their foliage colors range from burgundy to nearly black, chartreuse, deep purple, and light green to red, variegated (green with pink or white), and yellow, and their leaves can take on exotic forms, including three-lobe, heart-shape, and maple leaf. These cousins of the morning glory *(Ipomoea purpurea)* occasionally produce small, trumpet-shape flowers that are insignificant. At first frost, the plants go dormant.

Although sweet potato vine's root tubers can be eaten, consumption is not advised, as their taste is variously described as bitter, starchy, and unsatisfying.

Sweet potato vine is a tuberous-rooted tender perennial native to tropical America. It is winter-hardy in Zones 9 to 11 and grown as an annual elsewhere.

PROPAGATION

Purchasing tubers in the spring or overwintering them in a dry medium such as vermiculite or peat is each an option. (See "Pondering Peat Moss," page 22.) When eyes appear, cut the tubers into pieces, with at least one eye per piece. Alternatively, in early spring, poke three or four toothpicks into the middle (waist) of a sweet potato. Then suspend it on the toothpicks in a glass of water so that it is halfway submerged. It is ready for planting when sprouts appear.

Plants can also be started from cuttings. Take a vine cutting and remove the foliage, except for a few leaves at the top. Place the cutting in water. Roots will form at the leaf nodes. The cutting is ready to plant when a small clump of roots appears.

PLANTING

After all danger of frost has passed and daytime temperatures are consistently above 50°F, plant in potting mix amended with compost and/or aged manure; ornamental sweet potato vines are relatively heavy feeders. Add a slow-release balanced fertilizer.

CARE

Place in full or partial sun. Note that although plants are highly adaptable

SWEET POTATO VINE COMBINED WITH CALADIUM, COLEUS, COLOCASIA, ORNAMENTAL GRASS, AND LIVINGSTONE DAISY

to varying light levels, foliage color is enhanced in sun and diminished in shade.

Water to keep the soil evenly moist; excess moisture can cause root rot. Sweet potato vine can tolerate some drought, but if it wilts, watering it well should enable its recovery.

Apply a balanced liquid fertilizer every 2 weeks.

Sweet potato vine spreads when leaf nodes that are in contact with the soil send down roots. This can create crowding and choke out neighboring plants. To prevent this, prune as needed.

DISEASES/PESTS *(see pages 184–200)*
Diseases: Botrytis blight, Pythium root and stem rot, Rhizoctonia root and stem rot, viruses. *Pests:* aphids, cabbage loopers, flea beetles, root-knot nematodes, slugs/snails, sweet potato weevils, thrips, whiteflies.

RECOMMENDED VARIETIES

- *Ipomoea batatas* 'Ace of Spades': spade-shape, dark purple leaves
- *I. batatas* 'Garnet Lace': leaves emerge bright green, then turn deep red
- *I. batatas* 'Goldfinger': three-lobe, bright chartreuse leaves
- *I. batatas* 'Lady Fingers': deeply lobed, medium-green leaves with burgundy stems and veins
- *I. batatas* 'Marguerite', aka 'Margarita': graceful, cascading habit; lemon-lime or chartreuse foliage
- *I. batatas* 'Pink Frost', aka 'Tricolor': variegated green, pink, rose, and white foliage
- *I. batatas* Sweet Caroline series: generally smaller root systems; variety of leaf colors

TRAILING LOBELIA

Lobelia erinus var. *pendula*

I MUST HAVE FLOWERS, ALWAYS, AND ALWAYS.
–Claude Monet, French painter (1849–1926)

I f you must have flowers, too, trailing lobelia will not disappoint. *Lobelia erinus* var. *pendula* is a trailing cultivar that puts on its best show from late spring to early summer when temperatures are cool. It blooms in shades of blue, pink, purple, red, and white. When summer's heat and humidity roll in, this beauty takes a break. Foliage and flowering decline significantly but, with pruning and relief from the heat, may return in early fall

WIT & WISDOM

- *The genus name,* Lobelia, *pays tribute to Flemish physician and botanist Matthias de l'Obel (1538–1616), who (with Pierre Pena) in 1570 described a detailed new plant classification system based on leaves.*
- *Do not confuse with* L. cardinalis, *aka cardinal flower, a native wildflower with a spike form.*
- *The species* Lobelia erinus *is native to southern Africa.*
- *Beware: If ingested by humans, lobelia foliage may cause serious health problems.*

RECOMMENDED VARIETIES

- *Lobelia erinus var. pendula* **'Blue Cascade': true blue blooms over pale foliage**
- *L. erinus var. pendula* **Cascade Mix: blooms in shades of blue, lavender, rose, red, and white**
- *L. erinus var. pendula* **Fountain series: large, early flowers; 'Crimson Fountain' blooms in deep red**
- *L. erinus var. pendula* **'Sapphire': electric-blue flowers with white eye**

light aids germination. Water from the bottom to minimize the risk of damping off. Maintain a temperature of 70° to 75°F; seedlings emerge in 14 to 21 days and blooms appear in 4 months.

Lobelia tolerates most slightly acidic soil types, but transplants will do well in potting mix amended with organic matter. Good drainage is essential.

CARE

In warm to hot and/or humid regions, provide partial shade; where summers are cool or hazy, trailing lobelia can take more direct sun.

Water to keep soil evenly moist.

Apply a balanced liquid fertilizer every 2 to 3 weeks.

Pinch tips to keep plants bushy.

Cut stems back by half after its first major flowering to encourage new blooms.

To avoid midsummer dieback as heat and humidity set in, cut plants back to promote a fall bloom.

DISEASES/PESTS (see pages 184–200)

Diseases: Botrytis blight, damping off, Pythium root and stem rot. *Pests:* none serious.

for an encore performance. Look for heat-tolerant cultivars.

Trailing lobelia is a tender perennial winter-hardy in Zones 9 to 11 and treated as an annual elsewhere.

PLANTING

Purchasing seedlings is recommended. Starting from seeds can be difficult: Seeds should be sown in seed-starting mix 8 to 10 weeks before the last spring frost date. Do not cover with soil, as

TRAILING PETUNIA

Calibrachoa hybrids

**I LOVE TO LISTEN TO THE STARS AT NIGHT. IT IS LIKE LISTENING
TO FIVE HUNDRED MILLION LITTLE BELLS . . .**
–Antoine de Saint-Exupéry, French aviator and writer (1900–44), in The Little Prince

Ring out! Commonly referred to by its trademarked name 'Million Bells' and also sometimes known as "mini petunia" for its abundance of 1-inch-wide blooms and resemblance to that annual, trailing petunia belongs to the *Calibrachoa* (CAL-i-bra-KO-ah)—not *Petunia*—genus. If given the attention it needs, this plant will pour forth hundreds of colorful flowers on stems up to 30 inches long from spring to first frost. The colors of its blooms range from blue, bronze, magenta, pink, and red to violet, white, and yellow. The plant is well suited for hanging baskets and containers.

Trailing petunia is a tender perennial that is winter-hardy in Zones 9 to 11 and treated as an annual elsewhere.

PLANTING

Trailing petunias are hybrid plants that produce few to no seeds. Purchasing plants or growing cuttings vegetatively (from an existing plant, unless such propagation is prohibited by trademark law) is recommended. Take a 6-inch

RECOMMENDED VARIETIES

Numerous collections and series of trademarked trailing petunias have been produced, including the ones listed below. When purchasing, always be sure that you have the "trailing" type.

- *Calibrachoa* Aloha Kona series 'Pineapple': yellow flowers
- *C.* Cabaret series 'Good Night Kiss': pink-purple flowers
- *C.* Cruze series 'White Pink Eye': white flowers with pink throats
- *C.* Kabloom series 'Denim': blue flowers
- *C.* MiniFamous Neo series 'Vampire': red flowers
- *C.* Superbells series 'Lemon Slice': white-and-yellow pinwheel flowers

cutting that is flower-free and remove the leaves from the bottom half. Dip the cut end in rooting hormone and plant in potting mix. Provide bright light and warm temperatures (about 70°F) and keep the soil consistently moist; roots should develop in 2 to 4 weeks.

When planting purchased plants or transplanting cuttings, provide potting mix amended with compost and/or aged manure and peat moss (if desired). (See "Pondering Peat Moss," page 22.) If using potting mix that does not contain fertilizer, add in a slow-release formula at the time of planting. A pH of from 5.0 to 6.5 is crucial: This plant will not thrive in a soil with a pH that is outside this range.

Move outdoors when the threat of frost has passed.

CARE
Trailing petunias require full sun (at least 6 hours per day); while they tolerate light shade, their production diminishes as shade increases.

Water regularly to keep soil moist but not soggy. Trailing petunia is somewhat drought-tolerant but check it often in hot, dry weather by pushing a finger 1 inch into the soil: If it is dry, water enough to be damp to moist. Between waterings, allow the soil to dry out. Wilting can be a sign of root rot, caused by overwatering.

Fertilize every 2 weeks with a balanced product.

Pinch back tips to encourage branching and flowers. Deadheading is not necessary, as trailing petunia cleans itself.

In midseason, if desired, encourage new growth/rejuvenation by cutting back branches.

DISEASES/PESTS (see pages 184–200)
Diseases: black root rot, powdery mildew, viruses. *Pests:* aphids, spider mites.

WIT & WISDOM
- *Trailing petunia attracts butterflies and hummingbirds.*
- *Its foliage is naturally slightly sticky to the touch.*

CONTAINER PLANT CARE

VARIETY	TASKS ACCOMPLISHED	DATE

HANGING BASKETS

THINK OF THIS AS A MINI GARDEN.
–Mary T. Dial, American garden designer,
in Columbia *[South Carolina]* Metropolitan *magazine, April 2016*

Hanging baskets, with trailing flowers that spill over the edge, have a carefree, lush look. They are especially welcoming on a front porch or near the front door. If you're thinking about filling hanging baskets with flowering plants, choose wisely. You can spend a lot of money replacing the plants if you don't select the right ones.

In spring and summer, garden centers are loaded with expensive hanging baskets just begging to be taken home and enjoyed, but the price can

be daunting. Don't despair! If you make your own hanging basket in the first year, in following years you'll need only to add new plants. Do not underestimate how much

money this project can save you over the years.

BASKET BASICS

Plastic pots aren't fancy, but they are inexpensive and readily available. You may even have some tucked away in the shed or garage from previous years.

Wire baskets come in a wide range of sizes and shapes and enable you to plant into the sides of the basket to create a fuller effect. Visually, the wire practically disappears. However, wire baskets can be

tricky to plant and are harder to maintain because they dry out fast. These need to be lined with either coconut coir or long-fiber sphagnum moss, which adds to the cost. To save a bit on that ingredient, try using burlap instead.

By placing a piece of plastic with holes punched in it (for drainage) over the liner before adding soil to a wire basket, you'll help to keep the soil moist for an even longer period of time.

HOW TO MAKE A HANGING BASKET

Creating a handsome hanger is easy:

1. Add potting mix to your pot to within 4 to 5 inches of the rim.

2. Arrange the plants while still in their smaller pots until you like the look. Floral industry standards suggest three to five plants per 10- to 12-inch-wide container, four to six in a 12- to 16-inch-wide one, and six to eight in a container 16 to 20 inches wide. Remember, these are just guidelines; another school of thought suggests one plant for every inch of pot diameter—for example, 12 plants in a 12-inch-wide basket. Exceptions would include vigorous plants such as pelargoniums (commonly called geraniums) and fuchsias, for which five plants would be perfectly suitable.

3. Remove the plants from their small pots and set them close—closer than you might in ground but not touching.

They need room to spread their roots. Plus, if the roots get too congested at the top, water will not settle properly. Pack soil around the roots to fill any gaps, keeping it about ½ inch below the container's rim.

4. Add a slow-release fertilizer and, if desired, a small amount of polymer gel crystals at planting time—but do not overdo the gel crystals: 1 tablespoon is plenty for a 10- to 12-inch pot. This substance absorbs 200 to 400 times its weight in water and slowly releases it when the soil dries out, but it also takes up room in the pot when saturated, which in a rainy summer can lead to root rot. (See "Solving the Mysteries of Potting Mix," page 18, and "Fertilizing Container Plants," page 30.)

VERBENAS

'MILLION BELLS' CALIBRACHOAS

5. Water well to settle the soil, then hang it up!

CHOOSING PLANTS

Before shopping for plants, think about the amount of sunlight that your basket will get: Is it all-day sun, shade, or half and half? Also, be sure to consider plants' water requirements before you commit to flower colors and plant heights. It's easy to fall in love with a combination of plants that won't make good partners.

Don't limit yourself to only annuals; some tender perennials are perfect for use in hanging baskets. Your plant display does not have to be all flowers; foliage plants offer seasonlong color and texture and can be the star(s) of the show.

BLOOMING PLANTS FOR SUNNY LOCATIONS

■ **Bidens,** in the aster family, boasts more than 200 species and is a reliable seasonlong bloomer. Its bright, daisylike flowers come in classic yellow as well as bicolor, pink, and white varieties.

■ 'Million Bells' **calibrachoas** look like tiny petunias. These are the backbone of many preplanted hanging baskets because they are so reliable and come in so many colors. (See "Trailing Petunia," page 173.)

■ **Lantana** is a sun-lover that can take the heat and will bloom in multicolor sherbet hues all season long. The trailing variety (*Lantana montevidensis*) produces branches at least 18 inches long.

■ **Fairy fan-flower** (so named for its petal arrangement), is a favorite annual. A low-growing survivor that is heat- and drought-tolerant and pest-resistant, it pushes out blossoms all season long. Colors include true blue, pink, purple, and white varieties. (See "Fairy Fan-Flower," page 160.)

■ Garden **verbena** is a colorful, drought-tolerant annual that blooms in colors ranging from lime green and peach to pinks and purples. It can be overwintered in the house for use again in the following year.

■ **Wave petunias** produce a larger flower than calibrachoas, cascade more, never need deadheading, and come in a range of colors. The original purple variety is

BEGONIAS

WAVE PETUNIAS

known to grow 2 inches per day—or 5 feet over a season. Imagine baskets planted with Wave petunias that reach from ceiling to floor!

■ 'Profusion Double' **zinnias** form neat mounds that are covered with long-lasting blossoms that stand up to the heat. They are good filler plants.

FOLIAGE PLANTS FOR SUNNY LOCATIONS

■ 'Silver Brocade' **artemisia** has felty silver leaves and is a reliable, drought-tolerant, filler plant. Shear upright stems in midsummer to retain a low profile; new growth will fill in quickly.

■ **Licorice plant** has velvety silver, chartreuse, or variegated cascading foliage and tolerates poor soil, heat,

and dry conditions. (See "Licorice Plant," page 162.)

■ *Lysimachia nummularia,* **aka creeping Jenny,** is a spreading perennial that is often used as a drape in hanging baskets. *L. nummularia* 'Aurea' has golden foliage that changes hue depending on light level: In full sun, it appears brassy gold; in partial or dappled shade, golden yellow; in shade, lime green to soft chartreuse.

■ **Sweet potato vine,** an annual ornamental cultivar of the edible species (but with bitter roots that are unpalatable), has colorful burgundy, chartreuse, deep purple, nearly black, or yellow foliage. The colors develop best in full sun to partial

shade. Leaf shapes range from maple to heart-shape to deeply lobed. Store tubers in a cool, dry place in peat or vermiculite throughout the winter and use them to sprout new plants in the following year or keep vine cuttings in water until you're ready to plant them in the spring. (See "Sweet Potato Vine," page 168.)

TRAILING PLANTS FOR SHADY LOCATIONS

These plants perform well with less than 4 hours of sun per day:

■ The *Begonia* genus consists of about 2,000 species with seven different growth habits. *B. semperflorens,* aka wax begonias, bloom with single or double bicolor, pink, red, or white flowers all summer long

IMPATIENS

FUCHSIAS

amid waxy foliage that can be green or bronze. Tuberous begonias have beautiful, camellia-like flowers and stunning green or dark, almost black foliage. The "cascading" series drape naturally. Overwinter tubers in a cool, dark location to replant in the following year. (See "Palm-Leaf Begonia," page 109.)

■ **Browallia** will give you true blue (and purple and white) blossoms for a unique and stunning combination. Bells is the trailing series; Starlight produces dense, compact plants; the Troll series are compact and rounded.

■ **Caladiums** are tropical foliage plants that are spectacular for any shady location. Their multicolor leaves—combina-tions of green, pink, red, and/or white—will add drama to a basket. Leaves grow on petioles (not stems) from tubers (the larger the tuber, the more leaf buds) that can be overwintered when dry. For instant color, use started plants. (See "Caladium," page 141.)

■ **Coleuses** are classic shade plants, although now there are sun-loving varieties, too. Capable of adding lots of color and texture to any basket, types include the Fairway series, whose dwarf varieties are 8 to 10 inches tall; the Wizard series, with 12- to 14-inch plants; the Kong series, which produce large, showy leaves on up to 2-foot-tall plants; 'Black Dragon', at 18 inches; and the Premium Sun series, which prefer full-sun exposure. (See "Coleus," page 145.)

■ Pendulous **fuchsia** flowers evoke *ooo*'s and *ahh*'s, but behind the scenes these showstoppers are fussy. As heavy feeders, they require half-strength fertilizer every week, consistently evenly moist soil, and protection from hot afternoon sun. However, they are a hummingbird magnet! (See "Fuchsia," page 105.)

■ **Impatiens** are a favorite plant for shade because they are in constant bloom in so many bright colors. (Look for downy mildew–resistant cultivars.) Double-flowering varieties produce blossoms that resemble tiny roses. New Guinea impatiens can

PELARGONIUMS

COLEUSES

take more light than other impatiens (they especially like morning sun) but still appreciate protection in the hot afternoon; their attributes include handsome dark green or maroon foliage and seasonlong blossoms.

- *Strobilanthes dyerianus,* **aka Persian shield,** is an upright sub-shrub that will reach 5 feet if unbound but stays small in containers. Its foliage is a metallic silvery-purple (hence the common name) on top and dark purple underneath, although colors fade with time. A stunning centerpiece or focal point plant, it loves heat, humidity, and moisture (dry air causes its leaves to drop).
- **Wishbone flower** has both trailing and upright types. It constantly blooms in shades of pink, purple, white, and yellow in light shade but can handle some direct sun if kept moist. (See "Wishbone Flower," page 156.)

TAKING CARE OF YOUR HANGING BASKETS

- Watering is critical to the success of your hanging basket. During hot, dry weather, check the soil at least once a day to see if it needs water. Wilted plants can take a long time to recover. If necessary, dunk the whole pot into a bucket of water to revive it.
- Remove spent blossoms to encourage more.
- Fertilize regularly to keep your plant in flower.
- Hang the basket on a swivel connector so that you can turn the pot to keep it growing evenly.
- Some plants are aggressive growers that may take over your container. Don't hesitate to replant in midseason, if necessary. Pull out the offender or let it take over the pot and remove the others.

DETER THE BIRDS

If birds make their home in your hanging basket, you can make it less comfy for them by standing some sticks in the center, draping a plastic snake or a strip of fake fur to scare them, or adding a colorful plastic pinwheel that will spin in the wind.

181

OBSERVATIONS AND REMINDERS

ABOUT MY GARDEN

With hundreds of plants to "play with"—and suitable for any device, even your phone—
The Old Farmer's Almanac Garden Planner software makes gardening easier,
as well as more fun than ever! Try it for 7 days free at GardenPlanner.Almanac.com.

OBSERVATIONS AND REMINDERS

CHANGES TO MAKE NEXT YEAR

_____

_____

_____

_____

_____

_____

_____

_____

_____

_____

_____

_____

_____

_____

_____

_____

_____

_____

DEALING WITH DISEASES AND PESTS

Good news! Plants grown outside in containers or indoors often suffer from fewer diseases and pests than those grown in the ground. Should your potted wonders be attacked by troublemakers, however, don't despair! You can learn how to combat and prevent many common diseases and pests.

Each plant profile includes a list of diseases and pests that commonly attack that plant. Look up those diseases and/or pests here. If the given symptoms match those of your plant, you may have identified the menace. Follow these general guidelines and then consult each threat's "Notes" highlights. For further information, visit Almanac.com/Gardening/Pests-and-Diseases.

GUIDELINES FOR MANAGING PLANT DISEASES AND PESTS
- **Start with healthy plants.** Choose disease- and pest-resistant varieties. Select certified disease-free seeds/slips/seed potatoes, if available. Inspect transplants

before planting and discard any that have signs of diseases or pests. Do not save seeds from infected plants, as some (seed-borne) diseases (e.g., anthracnose) may survive in the seeds.
- **Use new container growing medium every year,** if possible, especially if soilborne diseases were prevalent during the growing season. Some diseases overwinter in the soil, as do some insects and their eggs.
- **Remove affected material.** Destroy infected/infested plant parts before they can spread to healthy tissue or other plants. If a disease or pest has been particularly virulent, dispose of the entire plant. In general, do not compost diseased or insect-infested plant debris. Most home compost piles do not reach a high enough temperature to kill pathogens (fungi, bacteria, etc.) or insect pests.
- **Remove insect pests.** Pick larger pests off plants by hand or with tweezers. Crush them and their eggs or drown them by dropping them into a bucket of soapy water.

- **Sanitize.** Cleanliness is the best defense against diseases. (See "How to Clean Containers and Tools," page 16.) Sterilize tools before and after you use them. To prevent spreading disease, disinfect pruning shears or other cutting tools with 70% isopropyl alcohol between each cut. When your garden tasks are done, clean soil from your tools, shoes, wheelbarrow tires—wherever it is attached.
- **Rotate plants** (if applicable) in 3-year cycles, at minimum, to deter diseases and pests from attacking new plants. If you must use the same growing medium in the following year, rotate crops or annual ornamentals with ones that are not from the same family (which typically are attacked by similar diseases and pests).
- **Weed!** Weeds may harbor diseases or attract insects. Fungi, bacteria, and other pathogens, as well as insects and their eggs, can overwinter in perennial weeds and volunteer plants.
- **Remove fallen plant debris regularly** and do a thorough

fall cleanup. Vegetative material may harbor disease pathogens, insects, or insect eggs. Some diseases survive over winter only on living plant tissue (including weeds, seeds, and tubers), while others can subsist in soil or dead vegetation.

■ **Mulch.** A light layer of organic mulch on the soil surface can discourage insects from laying eggs in the soil, as well as prevent water from rain or hoses from splashing soilborne pathogens onto plants. Mulch also helps to prevent plant stress, keeping the soil moderately cool and moist. Avoid having organic mulch touch stems

and be careful that the soil underneath does not become waterlogged; check for slugs and other critters. Synthetic reflective mulch in silver or other light colors can disorient certain flying insects, such as thrips, and discourage them from landing on plants. (See also "Caring for Container Plants," page 28.)

■ **Allow air to circulate.** To prevent diseases that prefer humidity, provide enough space between plants and containers to allow air to flow easily among them. When selecting a container site, determine whether trees, shrubs, buildings, or other objects will block air movement.

■ **Be water wise.** Do not water from the top of plants, especially during cool, cloudy weather. Instead, use drip irrigation, soaker hoses, or similar methods to help prevent leaves, flowers, and other plant parts from getting wet. This will deter the spread of diseases that travel via splashed water or prefer moist surfaces. (If applicable, train plants to grow vertically to help in preventing disease spores from splashing onto plants from the soil and soil-dwelling insects from accessing plants' upper reaches.) Water early in the day to allow time for plants to dry before nightfall, thereby discouraging moisture-loving pathogens. Allow water to percolate through the growing medium to help to prevent roots and lower stems from rot that is caused by diseases that prefer moisture. Avoid excessive or inadequate watering. Too much water can lower oxygen levels at the roots and encourage root rot diseases, such as Phytophthora. Too little water can increase plant susceptibility to other stressors, such as spider mites. (See also "Sunlight and Water Essentials," page 24.)

■ **Maintain plant vigor and avoid plant stress.** Plants that have the conditions and nutrients that they need are more likely to withstand attacks by certain diseases and pests.

■ **Avoid overfertilizing.** This can cause a nutrient imbalance, thereby making plants more vulnerable to attack: For example, excess nitrogen can encourage a flush of tender, young growth that may be susceptible to diseases and pests. (See also "'FOOF': Fear of Overfertilizing," page 34.)

■ **Invite beneficial insects.** Lady beetles, lacewings, syrphid fly larvae, parasitic wasps, and other beneficial insects prey on insect pests. Encourage them by planting their favorite native flowers nearby; avoid pesticides that can also harm beneficials.

■ **Plant companion plants.** When growing nearby, these can repel pests that attack another plant, attract beneficial insects, or, as trap crops, lure pests away from a prized edible or ornamental.

■ **Install protective covers over edibles.** Row covers, fine netting, or other barriers cut to size will help to prevent pests from accessing plants to lay eggs and feed, as well as curtail the chance of their spreading disease. Covers can also help to prevent the spread of disease via wind or splashed water. Remove covers when flowers appear to allow for pollinator access.

■ **Employ sticky traps.** Yellow or white ones can trap smaller flying pests, thereby helping you to monitor their populations.

■ **Apply horticultural oil or insecticidal soap.** These help to control certain soft-body insects and their eggs. Always follow label instructions.

KEY: B = caused by bacterium/bacteria; F = caused by fungus/fungi; O = caused by oomycete(s)/water mold(s); DNC = do not compost; V = variable

Anthracnose: F; favors wet conditions; spreads via wind/splashed water; may be seed-borne

Signs: V; yellow/brown/purple/black leaf spots may dry/fall out; foliage yellows/curls/drops; sunken stem/crown/pod/fruit lesions; dark specks or pink/orange gel in lesions; twig distortion/dieback; poor flowering; fruit/roots rot. On banana: dark brown/black lesions on developing fruit; fruit ripen prematurely or blacken/shrivel.

Notes: destroy infected parts (DNC); remove plant debris; good air circulation; avoid overhead watering/handling of wet plants

Aster yellows (aka "purple top" for potatoes): caused by phytoplasmas (bacteria-like microorganisms); transmitted by leafhoppers; may be seed-borne

Signs: V; stunting/distortion; leaves dull yellow/purple, may curl; flowers pale or green/produce leafy growth; witches' broom; plants slow-growing/unusually upright/stiff; plants may wilt/topple; carrots deformed/hairy; potato tubers soft/small; aerial potato tubers may form

Notes: destroy infected plants (DNC); silver reflective mulch; row covers; yellow sticky traps to monitor leafhoppers

Black (Itersonilia) canker: F; favors cool/moist conditions; spreads via wind; may be seed-borne

Signs: shallow, reddish-brown/purple/black cankers form on crown and/or shoulder of root crops; small, orange-brown spots on leaves w/ green halos; flowers rot

Notes: destroy infected parts (DNC); cover shoulders of root vegetables with soil; control carrot rust fly

Black Sigatoka disease: serious F; favors warm/humid/wet conditions; spreads via wind/splashed water; present in Florida/Hawaii

Signs: new leaves most susceptible; tiny, reddish-brown specks/streaks or dark spots w/ gray centers on leaf undersides enlarge/merge; yellow halos around lesions; may spread to upper surface; leaves yellow or brown/die; poor fruiting/growth

Notes: destroy infected leaves (DNC); good air circulation/drainage

Blight, Botrytis (aka "gray mold"): F; favors cool/damp conditions; spreads via wind/splashed water; may be seed-borne

Signs: V; yellow/brown/gray/white spots w/ water-soaked margins on leaves/flowers/fruit; leaf/twig dieback; gray mold; buds remain closed; flowers wilt/drop; stem lesions; fruit drops/rots; plants wilt/rot; small bulbs

Notes: destroy infected parts/severely diseased plants (DNC); good air circulation; avoid overhead watering

Blight, early: F; favors warm/humid/wet conditions; spreads via wind/splashed water; may be seed-borne

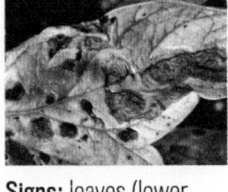

Signs: leaves (lower ones first) develop dark, concentric spots, often w/ yellow outer ring, and eventually yellow/drop/die; fruit/tubers/stems also may be affected; potato tubers develop dark, sunken lesions/corky texture

Notes: destroy infected parts (DNC); plant resistant varieties; rotate; remove plant debris; good air circulation; avoid overhead watering; harvest when plants are dry

Blight, halo: B; favors cool to moderate/humid/wet conditions; spreads via wind/splashed water; may be seed-borne

Signs: tiny, water-soaked spots on leaf undersides turn brown/dry out, becoming visible on upper surface; light green to yellow halo around spots; leaves distort/yellow; defoliation; spots on pods become sunken/red-brown, may ooze; red/brown water-soaked lesions on stems w/ white, greasy ooze

Notes: destroy infected plants (DNC); plant resistant varieties; rotate; weed; avoid overhead watering

Blight, late: O; favors cool to moderate/moist conditions; spreads via wind/splashed water

Signs: water-soaked, green/brown spots on leaves (youngest first), sometimes w/ greenish-gray/yellow halo; leaves brown/wilt/die; white, fuzzy growth on leaf undersides; black/brown stem lesions; greasy/water-soaked spots on tomato fruit expand/darken, turning leathery/firm and leading to rot; potato tubers develop brown/red/purple dry rot; plants die rapidly

Notes: destroy infected leaves/plants/fruit (DNC); plant early; rotate; keep leaves dry

Blight, southern: F; favors warm/wet conditions; may spread via splashed water; soilborne

Signs: leaves/stems/entire plants wilt, brown/blacken, and may die; water-soaked, brown/black lesions on lower stems; crown/bulb/rhizome/fruit rot; fluffy, white fungal mats with mustard seed-like

balls on stem bases/nearby potting mix

Notes: promptly destroy infected parts/severely diseased plants, white fungal mats, and surrounding soil to at least 6 inches beyond plant and 8 inches deep (DNC); remove plant debris; good drainage

Blossom-end rot: disorder caused by lack of calcium in fruit, often due to roots failing to obtain sufficient water and/or nutrients

Signs: dark, water-soaked spots on blossom end of fruit (opposite stem) may enlarge and become sunken/leathery

Notes: remove affected fruit; plant at proper soil temperature; mulch; provide good drainage; water deeply/evenly; maintain proper soil pH (around 6.5)/nutrient levels; avoid excessive nitrogen; prevent root damage

Cracking: disorder that in tomatoes is caused by fruit growing too rapidly for skin to handle, due to uneven moisture or high nitrogen, or skin expansion/contraction during fluctuating temperatures

Signs: from stem end, skin breaks radially or in concentric circles

Notes: plant resistant varieties; mulch; water consistently; maintain good leaf cover of developing fruit

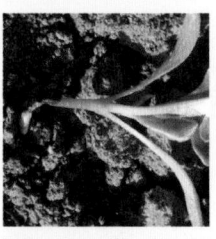

Damping off: F/O; attacks seeds/seedlings; favors cool/wet conditions (some exceptions); may be soilborne/seed-borne

Signs: seeds exude white substance/rot; seedlings fail to emerge or are stunted/mushy; seedlings darken/shrivel at/below soil line and topple/die; moldy growth

Notes: destroy infected seedlings (DNC); do not sow seeds too deeply; good air circulation/

drainage/sanitation essential; avoid excessive nitrogen

Leaf spot, angular (of cucurbits): B; favors warm/humid conditions; spreads via splashed water; may be seed-borne

Signs: leaves (undersides first) develop small, angular, brown spots, sometimes w/ yellow halos, usually between veins; clear/white ooze in lesions dries to white film; spots dry/drop out, leaving holes; fruit spotted/rot; vines/seeds also infected

Notes: remove plant debris; rotate; avoid overhead watering/handling of wet plants

Leaf spot, bacterial (aka "bacterial blight"; see also "Leaf spot, angular"): B; often favors warm/humid/wet conditions; spreads via splashed water; may be seed-borne

Signs: V; small, greasy, yellow/rust/brown/black leaf spots, sometimes

angular or w/ yellow halos, may enlarge/merge; leaf spots may dry/fall out; leaves slimy or yellow/distort/wilt/drop; stems develop blue-black cankers; vines wilt; flowers distorted; fruit blistered/spotted; roots rot; may have foul odor

Notes: destroy infected parts/severely diseased plants promptly (DNC); rotate; avoid overhead watering/handling of wet plants

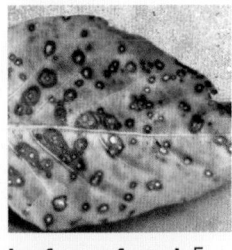

Leaf spot, fungal: F (including Alternaria and Cercospora); usually favors warm/humid/wet conditions; may spread via wind/splashed water; may be seed-borne

Signs: V; tan/brown/black leaf spots (lower, older leaves first), sometimes with purple borders/yellow halo, or reddish-brown leaf spots (upper, younger leaves first), sometimes w/ yellow halo; fuzzy growth or pustules may be in lesions; leaves die

Notes: destroy infected leaves/severely diseased plants (DNC); good air circulation; avoid overhead watering

Mildew, downy: O; favors cool/humid/wet conditions; spreads via wind/splashed water

Signs: V; yellow/brown/purple angular spots between leaf veins on upper leaf surfaces; onion leaf tips die back/yellow; downy, gray-white (sometimes purplish) growth on leaf undersides; defoliation; bulbs spongy/small

Notes: destroy infected parts or bulbs/severely diseased plants (DNC); good air circulation; water early in day/avoid overhead watering

Mildew, powdery: F; often favors moderately warm/dry days with cool/humid nights; spreads via wind

Signs: V; white spots or flourlike coating on upper leaf surfaces; leaves may yellow/brown, curl, die, and drop; symptoms

may also appear on stems/flowers/fruit; distortion/stunting

Notes: destroy infected parts (DNC); good air circulation; spray plants with solution of 1 tablespoon baking soda, 1 tablespoon vegetable oil, and ½ teaspoon liquid dish soap in 1 gallon of water

Panama disease (aka "Fusarium wilt of banana," "Panama wilt"): F, long-lived; spreads by contaminated water/plants/material; soilborne; present in Florida/Hawaii

Signs: usually infects roots first; roots/rhizomes rot; pseudostem splits/rots at core, with brown/black discoloration and possible bad odor; leaves (older first) turn yellow; plant wilts/dies

Notes: destroy infected plants (DNC); remove surrounding soil; plant resistant varieties; remove plant debris; disinfect tools/containers

Pink root: F; attacks roots of mainly onions; favors moderate to warm temperatures/ moist conditions; soilborne (to depth of 1½ feet)

Signs: light pink roots darken to red/purple/ black and shrivel/die; poor growth/stunting; leaf tip dieback; bulbs small/shriveled

Notes: destroy infected plants (DNC); remove surrounding soil; plant resistant varieties; rotate (3 to 6 years); maintain plant vigor; good soil fertility

Purple blotch: F; favors moderate to warm temperatures/humid conditions; spreads via wind/splashed water

Signs: older leaves first; small, oval, water-soaked leaf spots with pale centers enlarge to brown/purple streaks often w/ yellow halo; lesions may cover entire leaf; leaf tip dieback;

leaves wilt/die; bulbs small/rot in storage

Notes: destroy infected plants (DNC); rotate; remove plant debris; good air circulation; water early in day; avoid plant stress; control thrips

Rot, bacterial bud (of canna): B; attacks canna through its leaves; favors wet conditions; survives in rootstocks

Signs: white/black spots on young leaves; gummy sap oozes from lesions; older leaves distorted with brown/yellow spots; flower buds blacken/ remain closed; stalks or entire plants die

Notes: destroy infected plants (DNC); remove surrounding soil; good air circulation; avoid overwatering/overhead watering

Rot, bacterial (Erwinia) soft: B; enters mainly via wounds; favors warm/ humid conditions; may

spread via splashed water; soilborne

Signs: V; in clivia, yellowing of bottom leaves progresses until entire plant limp; dark lesions at base of plant, which rots; foul odor

Notes: destroy infected plants (DNC); remove surrounding soil; remove plant debris; good air circulation/drainage; avoid overwatering/ excessive nitrogen; control insect pests

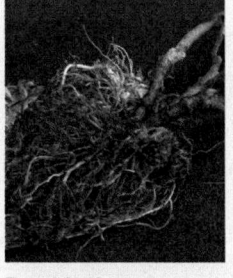

Rot, black root: F; favors cool/wet conditions and alkaline soil; many hosts; may spread via splashed water; soilborne

Signs: pale, yellow leaves; poor growth; stunting; plants wilt, especially in heat of day; dark brown/black lesions on roots; plants may die

Notes: destroy infected plants (DNC); remove surrounding soil; good drainage; avoid overwa-

tering/overhead watering; maintain soil pH at/ below 5.5; avoid plant stress; control fungus gnats/other insects

Rot, crown (of agave): F/B/O; often favors humid/wet conditions; may be soilborne; frequently introduced via wounds made by agave snout weevil

Signs: V; typically, lower leaves yellow/ brown; leaves develop spongy spots/wilt/ shrivel; symptoms show at central part of plant and expand outward; crown rots; plants die

Notes: if mild, prune off infected plant parts; otherwise, destroy severely diseased plants (DNC) and remove surrounding soil; plant less susceptible varieties; make sure crown is above soil line; good drainage/avoid overwatering; control agave snout weevil

Rot, Fusarium root: F; favors moist conditions; spreads via splashed water

Signs: V; lower leaves yellow/wilt; black, water-soaked roots; sunken, tan/reddish lesions on lower stem may have powdery/yellow mass; mushy roots/crown; plants die

Notes: destroy infected parts/severely diseased plants (DNC); good drainage; avoid overwatering/overhead watering

Rot, Fusarium tuber (of caladium): F; favors cool/humid conditions

Signs: mainly occurs during storage but sometimes during growing season; light brown discoloration on tuber base, darkening over time; rot progresses from base upward; tubers desiccated/chalky

Notes: destroy infected leaves/tubers (DNC); plant resistant varieties; store tubers in dry, well-ventilated location with temperature above 60°F/do not refrigerate

Rot, Phytophthora crown and root (aka "Phytophthora blight"): O; favors warm/wet conditions; spreads via wind/splashed water; soilborne

Signs: V; typically, dark green/water-soaked spots on leaves enlarge and turn brown; oozing brown/black cankers on crowns/stems near base; water-soaked spots on roots turn brown/rot; fruit spotted/shrivel/develop white growth; stunting/poor growth; plants wilt/die

Notes: destroy infected plants (DNC); remove surrounding soil; rotate; good drainage; avoid overwatering/overhead watering

Rot, Pythium root and stem (aka "blackleg" of pelargonium/geranium): O; favors wet conditions; spreads via splashed water; soilborne

Signs: V; plants stunted/yellow/wilt/die; poor growth; stem bases brown/blacken/soften; crown rot; roots discolored/rot; outer root tissue easily pulls off; bulbs turn brown/black and shrivel, turning hard

Notes: destroy diseased plants (DNC); remove surrounding soil; remove plant debris; good drainage; avoid overwatering/overhead watering; avoid excessive nitrogen; control fungus gnats/other insects

Rot, Rhizoctonia root and stem: F; favors warm/moderately moist conditions; may spread via splashed water; soilborne

Signs: V; yellow/brown, wilting leaves; reddish-brown lesions/sunken cankers on lower stems/roots; roots discolored/mushy; brown webbing; plants stunted/may die

Notes: destroy infected parts/severely diseased plants (DNC); remove surrounding soil; rotate; good air circulation/drainage; avoid overwatering; avoid plant stress; control fungus gnats/other insects

Rot, white: F, long-lived; attacks alliums; favors cool/moist conditions; may spread via splashed water; soilborne

Signs: leaves (older first) yellow/wilt/die; white, cottony growth at neck/bulb base, later with black, poppy seed–like particles; roots/bulbs rot; plant pulls up easily

Notes: destroy infected plants/bulbs (DNC); remove surrounding soil; choose certified disease-free cloves/sets/transplants; disinfect tools/containers

Rust: F (some require two hosts); favors cool to moderate/humid/moist conditions; may spread via wind/splashed water

Signs: V; orange or yellow pustules on undersides of lower leaves/stems; pale yellow/purplish/brown spots on upper leaf surfaces; foliage distorts/dies/drops; stunting; poor flowering; plants weakened

Notes: destroy infected parts/severely diseased plants (DNC); good air circulation; water early in day/avoid overhead watering; for fuchsia, destroy nearby fireweed (Epilobium)/do not place near fir (Abies)

Rust, white: O; not a true rust; prefers cool/moist conditions; spreads via wind/splashed water; soilborne/may be seed-borne

Signs: chalk-white blisters mainly on leaf undersides; small, yellow-green spots/

blisters on upper leaf surfaces; distortion/galls; stunting; flowers/stems may also be affected

Notes: destroy infected plants (DNC); plant resistant varieties; rotate; avoid overhead watering; weed

Scab (of cucurbits): F; attacks cucurbits; favors cool/moist conditions; spreads via wind/splashed rain; may be seed-borne

Signs: V; gray/brown/ pale green leaf spots, sometimes w/ yellow halo, become angular; leaf spot centers may dry/drop; deformed leaves; fruit develop corky lesions or small/ oozing/sunken spots that enlarge/darken and produce green-black velvety growth

Notes: remove infected fruit/plants at end of season; plant resistant varieties; rotate; good air circulation/drainage; avoid overhead watering/ handling of wet plants

Scab, common potato: B; favors alkaline soil and moderate to warm/dry conditions; may spread via wind/splashed water; soilborne

Signs: V; typically, tubers develop brown/rough/ corky spots that can be raised/shallow/sunken; lesions may enlarge

Notes: cut out blemished areas before eating; plant resistant varieties/certified disease-free potato seed; rotate; maintain soil pH of 5.0-5.2, if possible (unless other plants in pot, too); keep soil moist after tubers start to form

Sclerotinia white mold: F, long-lived; favors cool/wet conditions; may spread via wind/splashed water; soilborne

Signs: V; pale gray, water-soaked areas on stems/leaves/other plant parts; white, cottony growth, later with black particles; bleached or

shredded areas; crowns/ fruit rot; plants wilt

Notes: destroy infected plants/surrounding soil (DNC); plant resistant varieties; disinfect tools/ containers; good air circulation/drainage; water early in day; avoid overhead watering/ overwatering/excessive nitrogen; weed

Sweet potato scurf: F; prefers humid/wet conditions and soil rich in organic matter; may spread via wind/splashed water; soilborne

Signs: skin-deep, dark brown/purple/black spots or blotches on roots may enlarge in storage; roots shrivel; reduced shelf life but eating quality retained

Notes: remove vines after harvest (DNC); choose certified disease-free plants or cut slips at least 1 inch above soil line; rotate; avoid excess organic matter; weed out wild morning glories

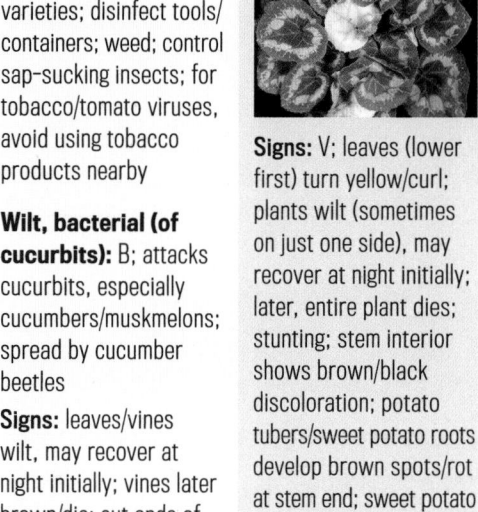

Viruses: caused by viral pathogens; common viruses include bean common mosaic virus, cucumber mosaic virus (aka "spinach blight"), lettuce mosaic virus, sweet potato feathery mottle virus (aka "internal cork"), tobacco mosaic virus, and tomato mosaic virus; often transmitted by aphids/leafhoppers/other sap-sucking insects; tobacco/tomato viruses can spread via tobacco products; some are soilborne/seed-borne

Signs: V; may include leaves with yellow/green mottling (mosaic pattern) or rings or brown/yellow spots, sometimes w/purple margins; fernlike leaves (tobacco/tomato mosaic); distorted leaves/stems/flowers; blistering; brown/black lesions; flowers streaked/discolored; poor flowering; warts on fruit; fruit ripens unevenly and/or shows browning; corky spots inside sweet potatoes (internal cork); stunting

Notes: destroy infected plants (DNC); plant certified virus-free seed/slips (if applicable)/resistant varieties; disinfect tools/containers; weed; control sap-sucking insects; for tobacco/tomato viruses, avoid using tobacco products nearby

Wilt, bacterial (of cucurbits): B; attacks cucurbits, especially cucumbers/muskmelons; spread by cucumber beetles

Signs: leaves/vines wilt, may recover at night initially; vines later brown/die; cut ends of wilted (not dead) stems, when pressed together for 10 seconds and pulled apart, release stringy, white to clear ooze

Notes: destroy infected plants (DNC); plant resistant varieties; disinfect tools/containers; control cucumber beetles

Wilt, Fusarium (aka "stem rot" of sweet potatoes): F, long-lived; favors warm/dry conditions and acidic/sandy/high-nitrogen soil; soilborne

Signs: V; leaves (lower first) turn yellow/curl; plants wilt (sometimes on just one side), may recover at night initially; later, entire plant dies; stunting; stem interior shows brown/black discoloration; potato tubers/sweet potato roots develop brown spots/rot at stem end; sweet potato stems bluish at soil line

Notes: destroy infected plants (DNC); plant certified, disease-free slips/resistant varieties; rotate; avoid excessive nitrogen/dry soil; in acidic soils, raise pH to 6.5–7.0

Wilt, southern bacterial (aka "Moko disease" for banana; "brown rot" for potato): B; favors hot/wet conditions; may spread via splashed water; soilborne; "Moko disease" strain on bananas present in Florida/Hawaii

Signs: V; leaves yellow/wilt, may recover at night initially; later, entire plant wilts/dies; stunting; fruit deformed/discolored/ripen unevenly; brown, sunken cankers at stem base; stem interior shows brown discoloration; roots rot; cut ends of infected stems exude milky ooze

Notes: destroy infected plants promptly (DNC); remove surrounding soil; rotate; disinfect tools/containers; good drainage

Wilt, Verticillium: F, long-lived; may favor cool to moderate temperatures/moist conditions; soilborne

Signs: V; leaves yellow and wilt (often lower first, sometimes on just one side of leaf or plant) in daytime/recover at night initially; later, entire plant wilts/dies; stunting; stem interior shows brown discoloration; poor flowering/fruiting

Notes: destroy infected plants (DNC); remove surrounding soil; plant resistant varieties; rotate; good drainage; weed

PESTS

Agave plant bugs (aka "running bugs"): 1/8-inch-long, narrow-body, brown insects with prominent eyes/triangular pattern on back; run quickly, hide in soil/debris; problem in SW U.S.

Signs: adults/nymphs pierce agave leaves to suck sap, causing pale yellow/white scars; leaves yellow/wilt; stunting/distortion; plants die

Notes: weed; remove plant debris; attract parasitic wasps; insecticidal soap

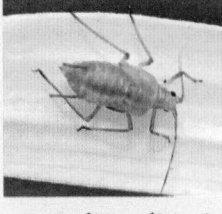

Aphids: 1/16- to 1/8-inch-long, antennaed, soft-bodied insects (some waxy/woolly; a few winged) of various colors; may transmit plant viruses

Signs: V; insects cluster under leaves or on stems/flower buds to suck sap from succulent new growth; misshapen/yellow leaves; distorted flowers; wilting; stunting/poor growth; leaf drop; sticky "honeydew" (excretion); sooty, black mold; galls

Notes: knock off with water spray/remove infested parts; weed; avoid excessive nitrogen; beneficial insects; check for pests regularly; horticultural oil/insecticidal soap

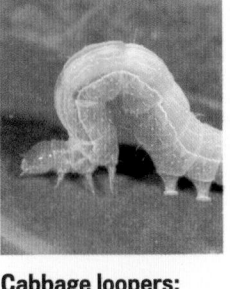

Cabbage loopers: smooth, white-stripe, pale green caterpillars, up to 1½ inches long, that move like inchworms become gray-brown nocturnal moths w/ white "8" or "V" on each wing; tiny yellow-white/greenish eggs laid singly

Signs: larvae chew large, ragged holes in leaves; defoliation; stunting; excrement; eggs on leaves

Notes: HP; weed; remove plant debris; beneficial insects; row covers; insecticidal soap

Canna leaf rollers: two types—larger canna leaf rollers (lime green, 2-inch-long caterpillars become small, brown, skipper butterflies w/ white spots; green eggs that later turn pink laid singly on leaves) and lesser canna leaf rollers (1-inch-long, yellow caterpillars become small, pale brown moths; pale yellow eggs laid in groups)

Signs: larvae of larger type roll up edge of a fully expanded leaf/secures with silk/feeds inside, creating holes and ragged edges; larvae of lesser type often target unfurled leaves/foliage chewed partially through; webbing; poor flowering; defoliation; excrement on leaf/ground

Notes: squeeze rolled leaves to kill larvae inside or destroy infested foliage (DNC); remove plant debris

Carrot rust flies: 1/5-inch-long, cream-color maggots become small, orange-head, metallic-color, greenish-black flies with yellow legs

Signs: larvae feed on roots of carrot-family crops, leaving tunnels with rust-color excrement; roots

deformed/rot; wilted/stunted plants

Notes: discard infested roots; rotate; weed; remove plant debris; beneficial insects; row covers; harvest blocks of carrots rather than just one or two at a time

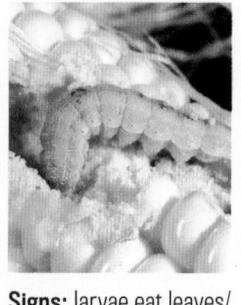

Colorado potato beetles: red-orange, humpback larvae with black spots become ½-inch-long, oval, yellow-orange beetles with 10 black stripes; attack solanaceous plants

Signs: yellow-orange eggs laid in clusters on leaf undersides; larvae/adults chew holes in foliage; defoliation

Notes: HP; rotate; weed; remove plant debris; straw mulch; row covers

Corn earworms (aka "tomato fruitworms"): pale-headed, variably colored, 1- to 2-inch-long caterpillars with white/dark stripes

and tiny black spines become moths that are usually yellowish brown; whitish eggs laid singly on foliage; favor corn but will also attack tomatoes/other plants

Signs: larvae eat leaves/silks and insides of flowers/fruit/pods; hole at base of fruit stem; excrement; leaves distorted; premature ripening

Notes: destroy larvae/eggs on leaves/infested fruit (DNC); remove plant debris; avoid planting near corn; beneficial insects

Cucumber beetles: two common types—striped (⅕-inch-long, yellow adults with

three black stripes) and spotted (⅕-inch-long, yellow-green adults with 12 spots); larvae are small, whitish grubs; orange-yellow eggs laid in groups; may transmit bacterial wilt

Signs: adults chew holes in leaves/flowers/stems; wilting/defoliation; rasped fruit; larvae feed on roots; plants stunted/die

Notes: HP; weed; remove plant debris; mulch heavily; row covers; monitor for bacterial wilt

Cutworms: large caterpillars that curl into a "C" become gray/brown/black mottled moths; depending on species, larvae may feed on either upper parts or roots/tubers

Signs: wilting; larvae sever stems of seedlings and transplants near soil line; whole seedlings disappear; holes in leaves

Notes: HP (at night); in spring before planting,

cultivate soil to reduce larvae; wrap a 4-inch-wide collar made from cardboard/newspaper around each seedling stem, sinking 2 inches into soil; weed; remove plant debris; row covers

Flea beetles: soil-dwelling, thin, white grubs become ¹⁄₁₆- to ⅛-inch-long, shiny black/brown/bronze/gray beetles, some striped, that jump when disturbed

Signs: larvae of most species feed on roots; adults feed on leaves/stems, creating numerous tiny holes in leaves; wilted/stunted plants if severe infestation; seedlings/young plants most susceptible

Notes: frequently hand-vacuum adults off leaves; weed; remove plant debris; mulch heavily; beneficial insects; row covers/fine screening during young plant stage; sticky traps

Fungus gnats: ¼-inch, clear to white, wormlike larvae w/ black heads become ⅛-inch-long, adult black flies; prefer moist conditions; may transmit fungal plant diseases

Signs: larvae feed on fungi/decaying matter in soil and may also feed on roots/lower leaves or tunnel into stems/ crowns; stunting; wilting; fine webs on potting mix surface; adults crawl on potting mix or weakly fly near plants

Notes: destroy severely infested plants (DNC); remove plant debris; good drainage; allow soil to dry between waterings; beneficial insects; sticky traps

Imported cabbage-worms (aka "cabbage whites," "cabbage moths"): slow-moving, velvety, 1-inch-long green caterpillars w/ thin yellow stripe along back become black-tipped, white butterflies with two or three black spots on each wing

Signs: larvae chew large, ragged holes in leaves or skeletonize them (only veins remain); excrement; yellowish eggs laid singly on leaf undersides

Notes: HP; row covers/ fine netting; beneficial insects; companion plants (including thyme as repellent)

Japanese beetles: C-shape, whitish grubs become ½-inch-long, copper-color beetles with metallic green heads

Signs: adults skeletonize leaves (only veins remain) and may also chew stems/ flowers/fruit; grubs feed on grass roots, causing dead patches

Notes: HP (morning or evening); attract parasitic wasps; plant tansy or garlic nearby; row covers/netting; spread diatomaceous earth around plants

Leafhoppers: pale, wingless nymphs become tiny green/ brown/gray/yellow/ multicolor, wedge-shape adults that can fly; insects hop or run sideways when disturbed; may transmit plant diseases

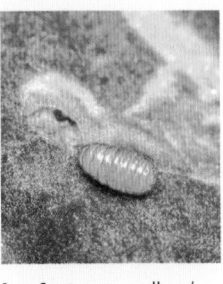

Signs: both stages suck leaf sap, causing stippling (many tiny spots); "hopperburn" (leaves yellow/brown, curled, or stunted); sticky "honeydew" (excretion); sooty, black mold or white, chalky film; white shed skins on leaf undersides (from nymph molting); reduced yield

Notes: knock nymphs off leaf undersides w/ water spray; weed; remove plant debris; silver reflective mulch; row covers

Leaf miners: yellow/ white maggots become tiny adult flies (often gray/ black); eggs laid in leaves

Signs: larvae tunnel in leaves, causing meandering blisters or brown blotches; leaves may brown/drop in severe infestations; damage usually only cosmetic

Notes: destroy infested leaves (DNC); rotate; weed; row covers/fine netting

Mealy bugs: many species; tiny yellow/ orange/pink nymphs become slow-moving, segmented, 1/10- to ¼-inch-long, oval adults, usually wingless and often covered by white/ gray, waxy fluff; favor warm/dry or indoor conditions; some may transmit plant viruses

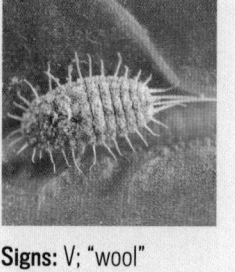

Signs: V; "wool" underneath/between leaves; nymphs/adults feed on plant sap; may attack leaves/stems/flowers/fruit; some species attack roots; weakened/stunted plants; yellow/distorted/wilting foliage; defoliation; sticky "honeydew" (excretion); sooty, black mold

Notes: HP; knock off w/ water spray; dab pests w/ cotton swab soaked in isopropyl alcohol; destroy severely infested plants (DNC); remove plant debris; beneficial insects; insecticidal soap

Mexican bean beetles: yellow, spiny grubs become ¼-inch-long adult beetles similar to ladybugs but copper-color with 16 black spots; attack beans

Signs: both stages feed on leaf undersides, causing "lacey," skeletonized foliage; yellow egg clusters on leaf undersides; dark holes on bean pods; reduced yield

Notes: HP; destroy eggs/severely infested plants (DNC); remove plant debris; white/metallic reflective mulch; beneficial insects; row covers

Mites, eriophyid (see also "Mites, fuchsia gall"): many species; microscopic, white/yellow, carrot-shape bodies with four legs; some may transmit viruses

Signs: feeding causes bronze/yellow/gray leaves that may be deformed/rolled; old leaves die/drop; some species cause galls/blisters on leaves/buds/flowers/stems, deformed buds; damage rarely serious

Notes: destroy infested parts/severely infested plants (DNC); weed; predatory mites; insecticidal soap/horticultural oil for severe infestations

Mites, fuchsia gall: microscopic/pale yellow/carrot-shape eriophyid mites that attack fuchsia; inject hormone as feed, causing distorted tissue and eventually galls in which they shelter; favor cool conditions; may spread via wind

Signs: feeding causes distorted/thickened/stunted young leaves/shoots/flowers; reddish leaves/shoot tips; galls (swollen, blistered growth); poor flowering/growth

Notes: destroy infested parts/severely infested plants (DNC); plant resistant varieties; weed; predatory mites; insecticidal soap/horticultural oil for severe infestations

Mites, spider: several species; minute, six-leg nymphs become tiny, eight-leg, hairy adults; prefer warm/dry conditions; may spread via wind

Signs: nymphs/adults suck cell contents, usually on leaf undersides; leaves yellow-specked, later brown-edged or bronze, and may distort/drop; buds/flowers distorted/yellow; plants die; fine webs

Notes: rinse plants w/ water; weed; remove plant debris; mist daily/avoid underwatering; beneficial insects; insecticidal soap

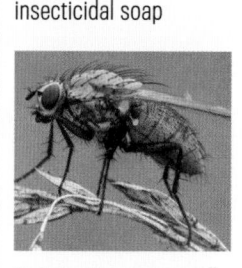

Onion maggots: small, cream-color maggots become ¼-inch-long, bristly, gray-brown, adult

flies with large wings; attack alliums; favor cool/wet conditions; may spread bacteria

Signs: larvae tunnel/feed on seedlings/roots/bulbs/stems, causing wilted/yellow/stunted plants; seedlings/plants may die; damaged onions rot in storage

Notes: destroy infested plants (DNC); remove surrounding soil; rotate; weed, especially wild onions; remove plant debris; avoid overfertilizing; beneficial insects; row covers; yellow sticky traps

Root-knot nematodes: microscopic roundworms that feed on cells in roots; favor warm soil temperatures

Signs: V; typically, roots "knotty"/swollen/galled; plants stunted/yellow/wilted/weakened; leaves/other parts may distort/die; poor flowering

Notes: destroy infested

plant debris, including roots (DNC); plant resistant varieties; rotate; disinfect tools/containers; plant French marigolds as a trap crop

Scale insects: many species; yellow/orange crawler nymphs become 1/16- to 1/2-inch long, oval to round adults; adult females of most species wingless/stay in place/protected by hard/cottony/powdery/waxy covering ("scale"); males, if present, are winged/do not feed; some species may transmit viruses

Signs: nymphs/female adults suck sap; leaves yellow/distort/streak/wilt/drop; fruit discolored; some species produce sticky "honeydew" (excretion); sooty, black mold; plants stunted/weakened/die

Notes: destroy infested parts/severely infested

plants (DNC); dab pests with cotton swab soaked in isopropyl alcohol; avoid overfertilizing; beneficial insects; insecticidal soap/horticultural oil

Slugs/snails: soft-body mollusks; snails protected by shell; favor cool/moist/shady conditions; active mostly at night or on cloudy/foggy days

Signs: irregular holes in leaves/flowers/stems; gouged fruit; slimy trails; seedlings "disappear"

Notes: HP (at night); weed; remove nearby debris; good drainage; water early in day/avoid overhead watering; copper plant collars; lure pests to drown in deep container of 1/2 inch of beer or of sugar water and yeast sunk to ground level; apply 1-inch-wide strip of diatomaceous earth

Squash bugs: small, green/gray, black-leg nymphs become 5/8-inch-long, dark gray/brown, flat-back adult bugs that often have orange-and-brown-striped edges; disperse quickly when disturbed; emit odor when crushed; yellow/bronze eggs laid in clusters

Signs: nymphs/adults suck plant sap from cucurbits, causing many small, yellow/brown/black spots on leaves; scarred fruit; plants may wilt/die; eggs on stems/leaf undersides

Notes: HP; crush eggs; remove plant debris; row covers; lay boards on ground/check for pests underneath each morning

Squash vine borers: 1-inch-long, cream-color, wrinkled larvae become 3/4-inch-long, orange-red/black, wasplike, daytime moths with olive-green front wings/clear hind wings; brown eggs laid singly at plant base

Signs: larvae bore into vines, causing them to wilt suddenly; plants die; mushy area and/or green to orange-yellow, sawdust-like excrement on/near stem base

Notes: if detected early, slit infested stem lengthwise to remove borer(s), then bury the cut in moist soil to encourage rooting; wrap seedling stems in aluminum foil collar; rotate; remove plant debris; beneficials; yellow sticky traps (for moths); row covers

Stinkbugs: bright-color (varies with species), oval, wingless nymphs mature to shield-shape green/brown bugs; hide when disturbed; some species may transmit plant diseases

Signs: nymphs/adults suck sap from buds/leaves/flowers/fruit/seeds; yellow/white blotches on leaves/fruit; scarred/dimpled/distorted fruit or pods; shriveled seeds; eggs, often keg-shape, in clusters on leaf undersides

Notes: HP (bugs emit odor, wear gloves); crush eggs; weed; remove plant residue; row covers; till soil in fall; insecticidal soap

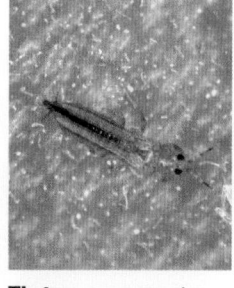

Thrips: many species; wingless nymphs become $1/20$-inch-long, slender, white/yellow to black/brown adults w/ fringed wings; may transmit plant viruses; may spread via wind

Signs: nymphs/adults feed on sap from leaves/buds/flowers/fruit, causing stunting/distortion and stippling/silver streaks; shoots discolored/rolled; leaves curl/drop; flowers fail to open; fruit scarred; black specks (excrement)

Notes: destroy unopened, infested buds/shoot tips (DNC); knock pests off with water spray; beat/shake branches/foliage/flowers; weed; remove plant debris; silver reflective mulch; avoid excessive nitrogen; row covers; sticky traps

Tobacco budworm: yellow/green/brown/red, often striped caterpillars, up to $1\frac{3}{4}$ inches long, become light-green/brown moths w/ cream bands and a $1\frac{1}{4}$-inch wingspan; white/gray eggs

Signs: larvae feed inside buds or on leaves/flowers/developing seedpods, leaving ragged holes; buds remain closed; ragged newly emerged leaves/flowers; black specks (excrement)

Notes: HP caterpillars (at dusk); plant resistant varieties; weed

Tomato hornworms: green caterpillars, up to 4 inches long, with eight V-shape stripes and black "horn" on hind end become large, mottled, gray-brown hawkmoths (aka sphinx moths) with orange-yellow markings that fly like hummingbirds; (tobacco hornworm larvae are similar, with red horn)

Signs: larvae feed on solanaceous plants; chewed leaves (initially toward top of plant); rapid defoliation; black/green excrement; gouged fruit

Notes: HP (at dusk; leave larvae that have white, ricelike cocoons, which house braconid wasp parasites); weed; beneficial insects; grow dill as a trap crop or basil/marigolds as repellents

Weevils, agave snout (of agave): Creamy white grubs w/ brown heads become ¾-inch, dull brown/black adult beetles that have snout;

favor agave; some of the larger species, such as *A. americana*, are the most susceptible; transmit bacterial plant disease

Signs: adult females bore into central leaves/plant base to lay eggs, also injecting bacteria to soften tissue for hatching larvae; larvae tunnel/feed into plant base; 1/8-inch-diameter, discolored holes in central leaves; leaves wrinkle/wilt; plant center mushy w/ foul odor; plant collapses/dies; bacteria spread to surrounding pups/agaves

Notes: destroy infested/dying plants (DNC); remove surrounding soil; HP weevils/grubs in soil; choose less susceptible, smaller varieties; avoid overcrowding; maintain plant vigor

Weevils, banana (aka "banana root borer"): plump, white larvae with reddish-brown head becomes 3/8-inch-long, shiny, brown/gray-black, adult weevils with snout; white eggs laid singly at plant base; nocturnal; present in Florida/Hawaii

Signs: larvae tunnel into pseudostem/rhizome/corm; roots destroyed; plants wilt/topple; poor growth/fruiting; young plants die

Notes: destroy damaged plant parts (DNC); remove plant debris; provide mulch to deter egg-laying at plant base

Weevils, sweet potato: wormlike, 1/4-inch-long, off-white larvae w/ pale brown heads become ant-like, 1/4-inch-long, black/metallic blue/orange-red adult beetles with snout; tiny, yellow/white eggs laid in roots/lower stems/entry hole plugged; favor warm/dry conditions

Signs: adults nocturnal/feed on all plant parts; larvae feed mainly inside roots; small holes/tunnels in roots, which may be spongy; tunneled stems; wilted/yellow leaves; plants stunted/may collapse

Notes: destroy infested roots (DNC); rotate; weed (especially wild morning glories); remove plant debris; mulch/mound potting mix around stems to prevent access by egg-laying adults; beneficial nematodes

Whiteflies: many species; tiny, often clear/green, wingless nymphs become 1/16- to 1/10-inch-long, flylike insects with white, waxy wings; favor warm conditions; some species transmit viruses

Signs: nymphs/adults suck sap on leaf undersides; yellow/silver areas on leaves; sticky "honeydew" (excrement); sooty black mold; distortion; wilted/stunted plants; adults fly if disturbed

Notes: remove infested leaves/plants; handheld vacuum to remove pests; knock pests off w/ water spray; weed; reflective mulch; beneficial insects; sticky traps; insecticidal soap

Wireworms: 1/4- to 2-inch-long, jointed, hard-body, shiny, brown, wormlike larvae or yellow/white soft-body larvae become 1/4- to 1 1/4-inch-long, dark-color, elongated beetles; adults click when righting themselves; favor cool/moist conditions

Signs: larvae feed underground; seeds hollowed; seedlings severed; stunting/wilting; roots eaten; tubers/bulbs bored

Notes: destroy infested plant parts (DNC); rotate; weed; remove plant debris; sow seeds in warm soil for quick germination; good drainage; avoid overfertilizing

DISEASE AND PEST RECORD

DISEASE RECORD	PEST RECORD

DISEASE _____

CONTROL MEASURES _____

_____

_____

_____

DISEASE _____

CONTROL MEASURES _____

_____

_____

_____

DISEASE _____

CONTROL MEASURES _____

_____

_____

_____

DISEASE _____

CONTROL MEASURES _____

_____

_____

_____

DISEASE _____

CONTROL MEASURES _____

_____

_____

_____

PEST _____

CONTROL MEASURES _____

_____

_____

_____

PEST _____

CONTROL MEASURES _____

_____

_____

_____

PEST _____

CONTROL MEASURES _____

_____

_____

_____

PEST _____

CONTROL MEASURES _____

_____

_____

_____

PEST _____

CONTROL MEASURES _____

_____

_____

_____

DISEASE AND PEST RECORD

| DISEASE RECORD | PEST RECORD |

DISEASE _____

CONTROL MEASURES _____

_____

_____

_____

DISEASE _____

CONTROL MEASURES _____

_____

_____

_____

DISEASE _____

CONTROL MEASURES _____

_____

_____

_____

DISEASE _____

CONTROL MEASURES _____

_____

_____

_____

DISEASE _____

CONTROL MEASURES _____

_____

_____

_____

PEST _____

CONTROL MEASURES _____

_____

_____

_____

PEST _____

CONTROL MEASURES _____

_____

_____

_____

PEST _____

CONTROL MEASURES _____

_____

_____

_____

PEST _____

CONTROL MEASURES _____

_____

_____

_____

PEST _____

CONTROL MEASURES _____

_____

_____

_____

DISEASE AND PEST RECORD

DISEASE RECORD

DISEASE ______________________

CONTROL MEASURES ______________

DISEASE ______________________

CONTROL MEASURES ______________

DISEASE ______________________

CONTROL MEASURES ______________

DISEASE ______________________

CONTROL MEASURES ______________

DISEASE ______________________

CONTROL MEASURES ______________

PEST RECORD

PEST ______________________

CONTROL MEASURES ______________

PEST ______________________

CONTROL MEASURES ______________

PEST ______________________

CONTROL MEASURES ______________

PEST ______________________

CONTROL MEASURES ______________

PEST ______________________

CONTROL MEASURES ______________

INDEX

Note: **Boldface** references indicate boxes or tables.

PHOTO CREDITS